WALTER'S
HORSE KEEPERS
ENCYCLOPEDIA

WALTER'S HORSE KEEPERS ENCYCLOPEDIA

W. H. WALTER
(Author of "The Right Way to Ride a Horse")

PAPERFRONTS
ELLIOT RIGHT WAY BOOKS
KINGSWOOD, SURREY, U.K.

NOTICE TO READERS

Every effort is made to ensure that 'Paperfronts' are accurate and that the information given in them is correct.

However, information can become out of date, and authors' or printers' errors can creep in. This book is sold, therefore, on the condition that neither Author nor Publisher can be held legally responsible for the consequences of any error or omission there may be.

Printed by C. Nicholls & Company Ltd.
The Philips Park Press, Manchester M11 4AU

CONTENTS

CONTENTS—*continued*

LIST OF ILLUSTRATIONS

Photographs in centre of book.

LIST OF ILLUSTRATIONS—*continued.*

Line Drawings, etc.

1
Breeds and types of horses and points

THE following are the principal breeds and types, under their recognised classifications. For photographs of them see the centre of the book.

HEAVY DRAUGHT HORSES

Shire. (Illustrated.) This is the largest breed in the country, the stallion averaging 17 hands in height, the mare slightly less, and weighing up to one ton. Not unexpectedly in animals of this size, both sexes are normally of docile temperament. Practically all whole colours are met, but chestnut and cream are not favoured, and the original black is becoming rarer. A feature of the breed is the profuse flat, silky hair, or "feathering" at the sides and back of the strong, massive legs.

The Shire traces its history back to the Old English War Horse, which claimed descent from the Chariot Horse of Ancient Britain; this original ancestor, a much smaller animal, was crossed with foreign stock to produce a massive steed capable of carrying the immense weight of an armoured rider, together with its own protective plating. Such was the noble descent of the dray-horse of more modern days.

Clydesdale. (Illustrated.) The Clydesdale might be called the Shire Horse of Scotland. It is, however, a lighter and more active type, ranging from 16 to 17 hands, and giving an impression of strength without unnecessary weight. The feathering, confined to the back of the legs, is finer and less plentiful than the Shire's. Whilst some chestnuts and blacks are found, the usual colours are bay and brown, with a white face or a blaze, and white legs from the knees and hocks downward, although the forelegs are sometimes dark-coloured. The face has a flat profile and the head is set on a long, well-arched neck.

This breed is noted for the wearing qualities of its feet and legs, possibly due in some measure to its fairly long, sloping pasterns, which reduce the effects of concussion. Another important characteristic of the Clydesdale is its free, elastic action, which makes it particularly suited for farm work, where a good, even and energetic walker is a great asset.

The breed has probably been built up mainly on a variety of Continental types, in conjunction with native Scottish breeds.

Suffolk. (Illustrated.) Lighter and more active than either the Shire or the Clydesdale, averaging only 16 hands, this horse is chiefly used in agriculture, being invaluable for slow work on heavy land, but is suited for a variety of purposes, having even produced excellent hunters when crossed with Thoroughbred stallions. The "Suffolk Punch", as it is commonly called on account of its build, can be instantly recognised by its massive neck, "square" body, and the absence of feathering except for a tuft of hair on the fetlock. It always breeds true to colour—chestnut—although this may vary in shade. A hardy constitution enables it to thrive where another breed would fail.

The origin of the Suffolk is uncertain, but there is no doubt it has been bred in East Anglia for about 500 years.

British Percheron. (Illustrated.) The Percheron originated in France and was not bred in England until after the 1914-18 war. Although easily distinguishable from the Suffolk Punch, it is similar in conformation, strongly built, wide and deep, but slightly taller; stallions should not measure under 16 hands 3 inches, mares not under 16 hands 1 inch. The head is large but well-proportioned, with full, docile eyes and an intelligent expression. Black and grey are the usual colours, no stallion of any other colour being accepted for the Stud Book. The Percheron has a reputation for activity and a capacity for long hours of hard work.

Light Draught Horses

Cleveland Bay. (Illustrated.) A large type of carriage horse, standing between 15 hands 3 inches and 16 hands 2 inches, the Cleveland was for long regarded as a "general utility" horse, working in stage coach teams, on farms, as vanners and under saddle. On account of its handsome appearance and reliability it is always sought for use in State carriages. As the name suggests, the colour must be a shade of bay, with black points and, of course, black mane and tail; there may be a dark stripe ("list") along the back. White on the legs or feet, or as a blaze on the face, may be regarded as indicating the presence of blood of another breed.

Like the Shire, the Cleveland sprang from the Great or War Horse of the fifteenth century, but since those days Thoroughbred and Arab blood have played their parts in its development. Now it is much favoured in the breeding of hunters and other saddle horses, usually being crossed with the Thoroughbred for this purpose. It was formerly used for work on light soils.

Yorkshire Coach Horse. (Illustrated.) This handsome animal is similar to the Cleveland Bay, but lighter and faster, standing between 15 and 15 hands 2 inches, showing more "quality" and having a higher action. Bay or brown, with black points, mane and tail, it breeds true to colour. The neck is well-arched and the head fine but slightly Roman-nosed.

The breed has been known in Yorkshire since the seventeenth century and has been carefully developed for more than a hundred years. Its history is closely related to the Cleveland's but includes a greater proportion of Thoroughbred and Arab blood, hence its more elegant appearance. Used in stage coaches at a time when faster animals were required for the lighter vehicles, it also made a first-class, high quality carriage horse, and has found Royal favour. In more recent years it has proved its value to farmers and has been successfully crossed for the production of saddle horses of many kinds, and especially for improving the native stock of other countries.

Hackney Horse. (Illustrated.) With its characteristic high action, well arched neck and great trotting speed, the Hackney is the most brilliant and showy of all our harness horses. To meet show ring standards, the natural gait has been developed to give shoulder and hock as well as knee action, the forelegs being well extended and "reaching out" before the feet are put down, the hindlegs well flexed and supplying the necessary propelling power. The Hackney Horse stands on powerful, short legs, and his height varies from 15 to 15 hands 2 inches, although now 16 hands is not uncommon. There are all colours, but greys are rare.

Although the breed has existed for over two centuries, it

is only of comparatively recent years that it has been recognised in its present form, the first Hackney Stud Book being issued many years ago. Its ancestors were probably the old "trotting mares" mated with Arabs. By reason of an ability to "go for ever" at its natural pace, the trot, it was a useful riding horse, but in present days its main purpose is show ring work.

Hackney Pony. Being closely associated with the Hackney Horse, this pony must be considered under the heading of Light Draught Horses. The same showy action is expected of the Pony as of its larger relative. In height it should not exceed 14 hands 2 inches, and chestnut, bay and brown are the colours most frequently seen.

Native ponies were used in its development, Welsh mares playing the largest part. As is to be expected from such blood, great endurance and courage, combined with docility, are features of the breed. The Hackney Pony should not be confused with the cob-type of Welsh Pony, which is quite distinct from it.

Saddle Horses

Arab. (Illustrated.) This beautiful breed could be summed up briefly by the words: "Quality, gracefulness and courage combined with docility and intelligence". In appearance it is distinguished by the small, neat head with dished profile, small ears, large nostrils and eyes, the arched neck and fine mane, and gracefully carried silky tail. The height rarely exceeds 15 hands, and the usual colours are chestnut, bay, white or grey, frequently brown, but seldom black. Anglo- and Part-Bred Arabs, as well as Pure-Breds, are registered by the Arab Horse Society.

This horse came to us from the deserts of Arabia and became the foundation of the English Thoroughbred.

Thoroughbred. (Illustrated.) The term "Thoroughbred" should not be confused with "Pure-bred". Strictly, it applies only to horses with both parents registered in the General Stud Book, and is synonymous with the term "Racehorse".

In former days, horses began their racing life much later than to-day when, for financial reasons, they are required to run as two-year-olds. This has led to a system of management whereby they are "forced" into early maturity, producing taller and faster *sprinters,* in many cases at the expense of stamina.

The usual height is about 16 hands, although some are under this and others exceed 17 hands. Colours vary, but chestnut, bay and brown seem to be most common, although there have been many good greys. The head should be lean and fine, with prominent, intelligent eyes, and the whole appearance suggest speed and alertness.

The modern Thoroughbred traces its descent back to three Eastern Stallions brought to England in the late seventeenth and early eighteenth centuries—the Byerley Turk, The Darley Arabian and the Godolphin Barb—but it must not be forgotten that other Eastern blood had been introduced before that time.

Hunter. (Illustrated.) Being a type, not a distinct breed, it is difficult to lay down standards for size and colour. In selecting a hunter, choice must be governed largely by the type of country; fast country calling for a Thoroughbred, and plough for a sturdier animal. The Thoroughbred takes a great share in hunter-breeding, many hunters being actually of this strain whilst others are the offspring of Thoroughbred sires and draught mares (particularly the Cleveland Bay). The inclusion of Arab blood is very desirable, transmitting, as it does, the stamina required to stand up to hardship; the tendency towards lightness in the leg rectifies itself after the first cross. What is needed is a horse that moves freely at all paces, can gallop on, jump confidently and stand up to work. Colour is, of course, a matter of individual preference, but light chestnuts and roans are least in demand. Some of our finest hunters are imported from Ireland, where the soil and climate appear to favour their breeding.

Hack. The term can be loosely employed to describe almost any sort of horse, of whatever shape, size or colour, ridden for pleasure, that is, hacking. It is frequently but ignorantly used in a derogatory sense. When considering the Show Hack, however, one must look for a certain, high standard. A small Thoroughbred, or an animal showing a good proportion of that blood, is favoured, not exceeding 15 hands 2 inches, and with good, free action. Given all the necessary qualifications as to conformation, quality and action, it will fail in the Show Ring unless properly schooled; perfect manners are essential.

Polo Pony. This is a pony in name only. At one time the height limit was 14 hands 2 inches, but now there is no restriction. It is usually of the well-bred Hunter type, and many good ponies have Welsh Cob blood. Some of our best Polo Ponies were bred in the Argentine from stock crossed with English blood.

Cobs. (Illustrated.) With the exception of the Welsh Cob, which is a distinct breed of pony, the term "Cob" refers to any animal between the heights of 14 and 15 hands, that is, between pony and horse size. It is also necessary that the animal be sturdy and strongly-built (hence the adjective "cobby" applied to a horse of similar build). The "weight-carrying cob", it is worth noting, makes an excellent Hack or Hunter.

Ponies

Connemara. The Connemara is a very hardy, compact, short-legged pony from the West of Ireland, standing between 13 and 14 hands. Grey is the most popular colour, with black, brown and bay slightly less common, whilst the original typical dun is not so often seen now; chestnut and roan are rare.

The history of the breed dates back several centuries to a hardy type of pony which existed in Western Ireland, the Connemara of to-day indicating the addition of Arab blood. The Connemara Pony Breeders' Society, formed in 1923, has successfully worked for the improvement of the breed by careful selective breeding, and to-day shows an encouraging increase in the number of registered stallions and mares. Recently there has been a good demand in England for Connemaras as children's riding ponies.

Dales (Illustrated.) The best description of the Dales Pony would be "a miniature cart horse"; in fact it probably descended from an original native breed of cart horse, and Clydesdale blood has been used for added strength and weight. The height does not exceed 14 hands 2 inches, and the favoured colours are black, bay, brown and grey, others pointing to crossing. Possessing great powers of endurance, it is generally docile and easily broken-in, and is equally suitable for riding or driving. The well-arched neck is short and thick, the back strong and straight, the legs and feet ideal, with a quantity of fine hair at the heels.

Its outstanding characteristics include sureness of foot and marked trotting abilities.

In its native dales it was employed as a pack-horse for the lead mines and as a farm worker; more recently, street traders and others needing a small, strong, hard-working animal, have discovered its value.

Dartmoor. (Illustrated.) The Dartmoor is popular as a child's pony when properly handled in the early stages and not corn fed (as with most ponies, oats make it difficult to manage). Its height should not exceed 12 hands 2 inches, and its favoured colours are bay, brown or black. The head should be small and clean-cut, with an appearance of intelligence.

Haphazard breeding, due to casual methods of turning out on the moors, has marred the breed considerably in recent years, but the Breed Society and other persons interested are working hard to restore the original type.

Exmoor. (Illustrated.) As a child's hunter, the smart-looking Exmoor is deservedly popular. Measuring usually under 12 hands 2 inches, it is a little weight-carrier. The head is small, with flat profile, wide forehead and nostrils, small ears, and the light-coloured muzzle, or "mealy nose", as it is appropriately called, which is a distinctive feature of the breed. There should be no feathering about the fetlocks. The colour most commonly found is mousey-brown, but there are some bays and duns. It is a native breed, claiming pure descent, but some authorities are of the opinion that Arab and Thoroughbred blood have been introduced, and its appearance supports that theory. Certainly, however, by judicious crossing, successful hunters and even racehorses have been produced from Exmoor blood.

Fell. (Illustrated.) There is little difference except in height, between this and the other hardy native pony from the Lake District, the Dales Pony, and in fact they originated as one breed. The Fell is the smaller, seldom exceeding 14 hands, the average being 13 hands 2 inches. The colour may be brown, black, grey, bay or dun, but never chestnut. A short-legged but fast, active animal, it is sturdy and strong, making a good ride and being well able to carry considerable weight. It carries plenty of mane and tail, and the silky hair at the fetlock is typical of the breed.

H.M. The Queen and Princess Margaret in former years

gained successes in the show ring with their Fell pony "Linnel Gypsy", a matter of some pride to Fell Pony enthusiasts.

Highland. (Illustrated.) The real Highland, or Barra, Pony hails from the Outer Hebrides; two other types (the Mull and the Garron) being offshoots developed by cross-breeding and better conditions. In its natural state the Highland rarely exceeds 12 to 13 hands, but in more favourable circumstances it attains up to 14 hands 2 inches. Though most colours are found, dun and cream are preferred, especially when accompanied by a black "eel stripe" along the back and dark points to the legs. The head is square, being broad between the eyes and short, but with wide nostrils and "dished" face; it has a pleasing appearance and is well carried on a strong, rather short neck. Its chief virtues lie in its gentleness, intelligence, sureness of foot and strength. A hardy constitution enables the Highland Pony to live out all the year round on indifferent pasture.

The heavier, Mainland type, is useful for weight-carrying over difficult country and for hill farm work, whilst the lighter Barra makes an ideal, reliable, child's pony besides being suitable for farm work and driving.

New Forest. (Illustrated.) The New Forest Pony is not an outstanding beauty; its general appearance, with short neck and fairly large head, is often described as "common". All colours are found, but mostly bay and brown. Sure-footed, easily broken-in and quickly becoming traffic-proof, the New Forest makes an excellent mount for a child and, at the same time, is a willing, useful harness pony. Living out on the Forest, fending for itself, it may not grow above 13 hands, whilst with better feeding and care it may reach 14 hands or a little over, but it should be mentioned, over-feeding, especially with corn, is inadvisable as it will soon "hot-up".

The breed is not now a pure one, other pony blood having been introduced, but records show that the original type was known in Saxon times.

Shetland. (Illustrated.) Probably the best-known pony in this country, the Shetland is the smallest and one of the oldest in existence. The maximum height for the Stud Book is 42 inches (measurement is in inches for the Sheltie), the average is 40 inches or less, and the smallest on record 26 inches. At one time there was a theory that, if bred and reared under less rigorous conditions, it would become taller, but this has not been borne out in practice. Almost every colour is met, but white is uncommon, and white markings are not liked.

The Shetland is often condemned as being "a little devil", but well broken and *sensibly* treated it will make a good pony for a child; it is surefooted, intelligent and docile, yet has pluck and is exceptionally strong. The head is fine and small, the body compact, and the mane, forelock and tail long and profuse. Almost as much a characteristic of appearance as the small stature is the thick, long coat. Foals, in winter, are especially well protected against the bitterest weather by a dense woolly undercoat kept dry by an outer coat of long hair. The Shetland is also remarkable for its long life, many attaining the age of 40 years.

The history of the breed dates back to the earliest times, and the purity of the type throughout the centuries is obviously due to the isolated position of its native home. It was at one time in great demand as a pit pony for deep-working coal mines, but now it is mostly used under saddle.

Welsh Cob. (Illustrated.) This is a very strong, ride-and-drive type, short-legged and a fast trotter, varying in height from slightly under 14 up to 15 hands, with silky mane and heel tufts. There are many colours, but more bays, browns and greys, skewbalds and piebalds being disliked.

The breed has been evolved from the native Mountain Pony, which it closely resembles, through the "Old Welsh Cart Horse", by many crosses, including the Thoroughbred. The trotting action seems to point to some Hackney or English Roadster influence. Though making an excellent harness horse, the mare can be used in breeding good Polo Ponies, and the stallion has been much in demand abroad for breeding military horses.

The uses of a Cob of this type are obvious and almost unlimited.

Welsh Mountain Pony. (Illustrated.) This hardy, spirited little animal is a native breed with a remarkable resemblance to the Arab. Though seldom exceeding 12 hands, it can easily cope with heavy weights, in saddle or harness, and shows great endurance. As in the Welsh Cob, the usual colours are grey, brown and bay, with the same exception to skewbald and piebald. With its appearance character and good movement, the Welsh Mountain Pony makes an excellent ride, but is particularly valuable for crossing out to breed quality ride-and-drive ponies, a Welsh-Arab cross especially producing good results. Difficult as it is to favour one native breed above another, there is little doubt that the Welshman should head the list for general qualities.

Welsh Pony. Between the Mountain Pony and the Welsh Cob there are two intermediate types of "Welsh Pony": the "Cob-Pony" and the riding pony. Both have the power of endurance, pluck and spirit of all Welsh stock, and are found in similar colours. The Cob type, evolved from the Mountain Pony and the Welsh Cob, ranges from 12 to 14 hands in height, whilst the riding type, produced from Mountain mares by Thoroughbreds and Arabs, does not exceed 13 hands 2 inches.

The number of horses used in Agriculture has continued to fall in the last few years, whilst the thoroughbred industry, despite financial difficulties, has gone from strength to strength. However, the majority of horses in Great Britain are used solely for riding, and the staggering increase in their numbers recently allows no argument as to their popularity.

The horse has no equal as a pet for pleasure and recreation.

2
Buying a horse or pony

THERE is no subject on which most of us feel the need for advice as on that of buying an animal, and there are few on which it is more difficult to give it.

Having decided the type required, advice sought should be limited to the suitability of a particular horse or pony for the work, its soundness and general health, and the reasonableness of its price. I am a great believer in first impressions, or "taking a liking" to an animal, and consider that the prospective purchaser is the only person qualified to judge in this respect—expert advice from a Veterinary Surgeon is essential, and should follow the selection of a likely horse before its actual purchase.

Mediums of Purchase. Buying a horse is a simple matter—as well as being most difficult. The advertisement columns of appropriate journals swarm with offers. Frequently the owner is "going abroad"; he may well be, but my suspicious mind becomes even more suspicious—I prefer the seller to stay in this country, where he can be found again if need be. When studying advertisements, be guided not so much by what is said as by what is left *unsaid*. A horse always assumes outstanding virtues when he is put up for sale, such a paragon he becomes that we marvel the owner can bear to part with him. Unfortunately, of course, he is often forced to—he is "going abroad". However, doubtful cases are comparatively rare now and editors are very careful about their advertisers; do not think that no advertiser is to be trusted—I have sold many horses this way myself and been reluctant to part with them!

It may be that a friend, or a friend of a friend, has, or knows of, a horse for sale. As a general rule such mediums are to be avoided if friendship is valued.

At the recognised horse sales there is usually a good selection, but the difficulty here is that it is not always possible to try an animal, and very sound judgment is required.

There remains, then, the much-abused dealer. Strangely, I prefer this medium to all others. Horse-dealers, like any other businessmen, have their reputation to consider if they deal in a large way. It is the "here to-day and gone to-morrow" type of which you should beware, but remember the dealer *is* a businessman and is not working for his health. Find a reliable man, preferably on recommendation, tell him what you want and how much you intend paying, and he will usually do his best to satisfy you. Perhaps I have been lucky, but I have never yet had cause to regret a purchase from a dealer, relying purely on my own judgment without the assistance of a veterinary surgeon.

I will not deal here with the examination of a prospective purchase. This cannot be taught in a hundred books, and is a task for your particular expert adviser. If you know little about horses do not pretend knowledge; you may have heard the legs should be felt, but unless you know what you are feeling for you will be as wise as when you started and will have displayed your ignorance immediately. The Veterinary notes in this book should help you in an examination.

Trial. Many advertisers and dealers offer horses with "any reasonable trial" or "on a week's trial". This is what you want. If you are a horseman of some experience you will probably be able to judge quite well by seeing the horse in his stable, by having him walked into the yard and trotted up, and then finally riding or driving him for a short time. With a week's trial you are much safer, but make allowances for new surroundings and different handling, do not judge him before he has had a day or two to settle down. During this time you can have your veterinary surgeon look him over. Then try him at the work expected of him, but be sure you are handling him in the way a horse should be handled—be completely fair, and give him every chance.

Veterinary Certificates. A horse may be bought "with vet's certificate", that is to say, a certificate as to his soundness, age, etc., but it is better to have an examination made by your own professional man. Remember it is not possible even for the expert to detect everything—an unsoundness or a disease may be present but undeveloped, or intermittent and not obvious at the time of examination.

Warranty. A warranty is a statement, either verbally or

in writing, as to soundness or suitability for the purpose required. The former, of course, carries less weight than the latter and may be resisted in the event of legal action. Litigation is at all times an undesirable procedure, but especially in the matter of horses where the ramifications are so intricate. "Caveat emptor" (let the purchaser beware) is the watchword.

When taking a written warranty, see that it covers everything with which you are concerned—age, freedom from vice, suitability for the purpose, as well as soundness in wind, limb and sight. It may be that absolute soundness is not so important as other points, such as freedom from vice in a child's pony—but this latter should be covered by warranty of its suitability as such. Note that "ridden by a girl", "driven in harness", etc., mean little and do not warrant its fitness for such purposes. "Believed sound" also carries little weight and can only be taken as an expression of opinion, not a warranty. A warranty does not cover obvious defects unless they have been specifically discussed during the examination.

Example of Form of Warranty:

Received from Mr. A. N. Other, the sum of £300 (Three hundred pounds) for a bay mare by Golightly, 15 hands, warranted 6 years old, sound, free from vice and quiet to ride.

Signed ....

It should be noted that the warranty consists of the description following the word "warranted"; thus, had this form read "......... hands, 6 years old and sound, warranteed free from vice and quiet to ride", age and soundness would not have been warranted.

Unsoundness. Within certain limits, this may be taken as meaning any disease or defect which is likely to detract from an animal's usefulness.

Value of Horses. Perhaps the less said on this subject, the better. The value of a horse depends upon its usefulness to the owner; an expensive show-ring animal may be worth nothing in a riding school, a hack worth its weight in gold to a riding master may not be worth a passing glance from the showing fraternity, and so on. Generally speaking, a horse is at its best between the ages of 5 and

10 years; its useful life may vary from 20 to 30 years, according to constitution, treatment and purpose.

Payment. Terms of payment will be arranged with the seller—deposit on concluding the deal, payment on or before dispatch, etc.—but normally the purchaser meets carriage charges and the cost of a veterinary certificate. Payment by the instalment system is also widely used through the services of well known hire purchase finance companies. Should instalment facilities be offered to you by the owner at his personal risk, you could rest assured he had faith in his animal and wanted a good home for it.

3
Teeth and ageing

Signs of Age. The outward appearance of the horse itself is a poor guide to its age; many old horses, from good treatment, appear much younger—and, of course, the reverse applies. It is frequently said that deepening of the hollows above the eyes is an indication of advancing years, but this, apart from being very vague, is also unreliable. Up to 8 years, age may be estimated with some accuracy from the teeth (after much experience) by the time of eruption, wear and general appearance. After this only a rough calculation is possible.

Terms in Ageing. All Thoroughbreds have their "official birthday" on the 1st January, others in this country on the 1st May.

The term "rising" means approaching; for example, "rising 6" is "nearer 6 than 5"; "off" means passed, thus, "5 off" is "over 5 but not rising 6". A horse is said to be "aged" when he is over 8 years old.

Other terms in ageing are:—

Colt:	A young entire (uncastrated) horse; racehorses up to 3 years.
Entire:	An ungelded horse, a colt or a stallion.
Filly:	A young female horse.
Foal and Yearling:	The first is a young horse of either sex (thus "filly foal" and "colt foal"), usually under one year, when it becomes a yearling.
Gelding:	A neuter horse. (A male, but castrated.)
Horse:	The general term for an animal of either sex, but strictly meaning a stallion.
Mare:	A female horse over 3 years.

Number of Teeth. The adult horse has 40 or 42 teeth, the mare 36 or 38. The variations are due (*a*) to the presence or absence of small "wolf" teeth in the molars, and (*b*) to the normal absence of canine teeth or tushes in the mare.

The formulæ are:—

Horse:	*Incisors*	*Canines*	*Molars*	*Total*
Top Jaw	3 each side	1 each side	6 each side	20
Lower Jaw	3 each side	1 each side	6 each side	20
Mare:				
Top Jaw	3 each side	—	6 each side	18
Lower Jaw	3 each side	—	6 each side	18

The Incisors are the nipping teeth in front, the centre two being the Centrals, the next the Laterals, the last the Corners. Behind the Corner Incisor is the Canine or Tush; the Molars following are the "Grinders" or "Cheek Teeth".

The Parts of the Teeth.

Fang: The hollow root within the jaw.

Fanghole: The cavity in the fang.

Neck: The meeting place of gum and tooth.

Crown: The visible portion above the gum.

Table: The wearing or biting surface.

Mark: A blackened depression in the table of the Incisors, which grows out with the wear of the tooth, serving as an indication of age.

Estimating Age. For purposes of ageing, the lower Incisors are observed; the mark is shallower in these than in the upper Incisors and therefore grows out sooner. Changes in the tables of the Centrals show a year later in the Laterals, and the following year in the Corners.

TABLE OF ERUPTION AND CHANGES IN THE INCISORS

Temporary Teeth: The milk teeth are small and white, with a pronounced neck, and appear as follows:

Birth or soon after: The two Centrals appear in each jaw.

4 to 8 weeks. The two Laterals appear in each jaw.

8 to 10 months. The two Corners appear in each jaw.

12 months. All temporary teeth are in wear.

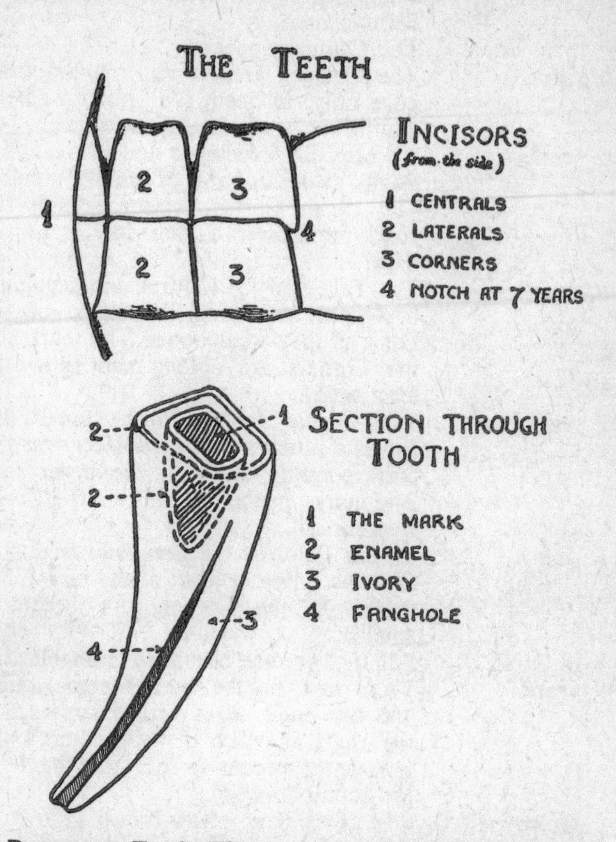

Permanent Teeth: The permanent teeth are larger than the temporaries, not so white and without a definite neck.

2¼ to 2½ years.	The Permanent Centrals begin to replace the Temporary Centrals.
Rising 3.	The Incisors in both jaws meet at the front edges when the mouth is closed.
3 years.	The Permanent Centrals are in wear.
3½ years.	The Permanent Laterals appear.
4 years.	Laterals and Centrals are level and in wear at the front edges; the Mark extends across the Table.

4½ years.	The Corner milk teeth are replaced by Permanents.
4 to 5 years.	The Canines appear.
5 years.	The Corners are in wear on the front edge only; all teeth are present and the mouth has a neat appearance.
6 years.	All are fully developed and in wear, the marks in the Centrals becoming smaller. The Upper Corner Incisor extends beyond the Lower Corner Incisor at the back.
Rising 7.	The Tables of the Centrals are becoming triangular, assuming the shape of the Fang as they wear down. The marks on the Corners are oblong and show the least wear.
7 years.	The Corner Incisor in the upper jaw shows a notch where it projects over the corresponding tooth in the lower jaw. The marks in the Laterals show signs of wearing out.
Rising 8.	In the Centrals the Fanghole begins to show as a line in front of the mark. The marks in the Corners are becoming smaller.
8 to 8 off.	All Incisors are becoming triangular.
9 years.	From now on the teeth become longer and lose their neat, vertical appearance, the angle at which the upper and lower jaws meet becoming less and the teeth projecting forward.

Galvayne's Groove. This is a yellow-brown groove on the outside of the Upper Corner Incisor, which starts from the gum and grows downwards with age. It is not seen in all horses, but when present is a rough guide from 10 years onwards.

10 years.	Galvayne's Groove appears.
15 to 16 years.	It extends from the gum to half way down the tooth.
20 to 21 years.	It is the full length of the tooth.
25 years.	The mark is half grown out, i.e., it is seen in the lower half of the tooth only.
30 years.	The mark disappears.

4
Stables and fittings

UNFORTUNATELY, particularly at present, the majority of horse-owners have either to make do with whatever stabling is available, or with buildings which can be adapted. This fact need not, however, prevent us from considering the form stabling should take, which will help when deciding the suitability or otherwise of existing buildings and how they can be converted.

Before commencing building operations or alterations, consult your local Council as to their requirements under Bye Laws, The Public Health Acts and The Town Planning Act.

Obviously brick, stone or concrete are the best materials, although they are better lined with wood as they are liable to be damp and cold, but timber stables, with walls not less than one inch thick, are very suitable. Concrete breeze slabs, faced with cement, are excellent and cheap building materials. Corrugated iron can be used if nothing else is available, but, if possible, should be lined with wood as metal has the disadvantage of being cold in winter and hot in summer, to say nothing of being extremely noisy in heavy rain or hail storms.

The best roofing materials are slates or tiles, especially when laid on a felted wooden roof, but matchboarding covered with heavy roofing felt alone is a good substitute, although it may need occasional attention for tears, etc. Thatch, whilst excellent as a non-conductor of heat, adds to the risk of fire and also harbours insects, apart from the fact that the art of good thatching is now nearly dead. Corrugated iron, again, is poor roofing; in addition to its drawbacks already mentioned, there is the objection of dampness from condensation. Asbestos is good from the point of view of reducing fire risks and extremes of temperature, but it cracks easily. Feather-edge boarding is suitable only for temporary shelters since it is never completely weather-proof.

Every effort should be made to provide each horse with a loose-box, that is, a separate "room" where it is at liberty to move freely in the space allowed instead of being tied up staring at a blank wall all the time it is inside, as in a stall. The loose-box, with its half-doors, also has the advantage of allowing its occupant to gaze upon the outside world—a horse is, or should be, of an inquisitive turn of mind, always interested in what is going on around it. Boredom is a great enemy in the stable, leading quite frequently to crib-biting, wind-sucking and other similar stable vices.

A loose-box must be large enough for the animal to turn comfortably without knocking itself, and to lie down and get up with ease and no fear of being "cast", that is, unable to rise when down. Once let a horse find it has difficulty in getting up and the chances are it will be reluctant to lie down again and will not get the necessary amount of rest. As a guide, a loose-box should be not less than 10 feet square for a 15 hand horse, with the doorway at least 8 feet high and sufficiently wide that there is no danger of knocking or brushing against the jambs when being led in or out—say 4 feet 6 inches wide.

In height, a stable with a span or couple-roof (that is, with two slopes meeting at a ridge) should be a minimum of 8 feet to the eaves; one with a lean-to (one slope) roof, 9 feet 6 inches at the front, which, with the least pitch or slope, will give a height of 6 feet 6 inches at the back wall of a 10 feet box. This last height is really too little, but to increase it would mean raising the front wall to an unusual measurement; therefore a span-roof is much to be preferred.

The partitions between boxes should be about 5 feet high, to allow the horses to see each other—often a great help in avoiding "boredom-vices"—and to assist in ventilation without draughts. They should, however, be barred or netted above this height so that biting is not possible.

That a stable is cold matters less than that it should be free from draughts. Here, of course, the all-important question of ventilation arises. Gone for ever, it is to be hoped, is the old idea that a horse must be kept in a sort of hot-house atmosphere, particularly at night. The necessity of a constant supply of pure fresh air cannot be too strongly

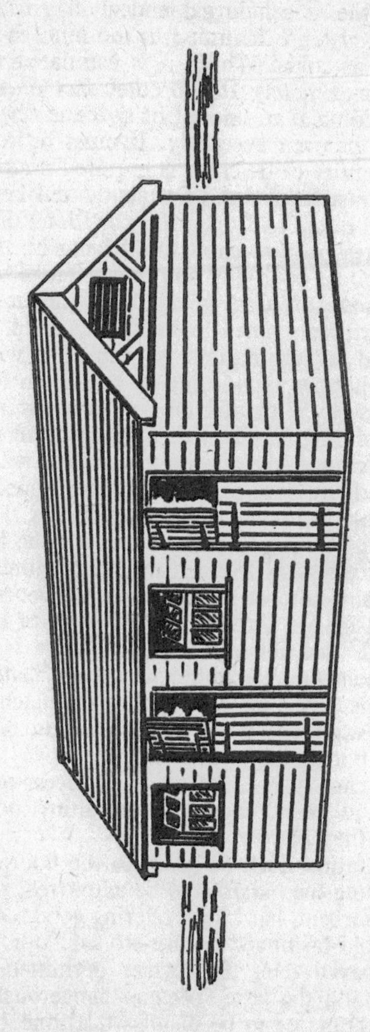

A RANGE OF LOOSE-BOXES.

Showing half-doors, hopper-type windows and louvre ventilation in end wall.

(Courtesy of Gregorys Sectional Buildings, Ltd., Uxbridge)

stressed; a stuffy stable is a fruitful source of colds and other ailments. Ammonia, which is produced in large quantities in a stable, is a light gas and quickly fouls the atmosphere, and bad air is irritating to the mucous membranes and leads to colds. Whilst it is estimated that a horse uses up approximately 16,000 cubic feet of air per hour, merely providing that amount of space is obviously neither sufficient nor even necessary. It must be remembered that this quantity of fresh air is required hourly and therefore the air must be changed frequently and kept circulating. With half-doors and open-top partitions this is a simple matter; unless rain or snow are driving in, the top door should always be open day and night. There will be times, in this climate of ours, when top doors must be closed, and against such times there will have to be an alternative method of ventilation. An opening window, preferably of the hopper type—that is, hinged to fall inwards—is the answer. With this type of window the incoming current of air is directed upwards and, being cooler and heavier than the air in the stable, will then descend and in so doing become diffused and warmed, thus avoiding a draught. If louvre ventilation at the ridge of the roof can also be arranged, as an outlet for the lighter, foul air, this is excellent as free circulation is more easily ensured. Light, being almost as important as ventilation, adds a further reason for windows in the event of the top doors being closed. (See illustration, page 21.)

A point to remember here is that windows, fastenings, electric light fittings, etc., should be well out of reach of the horse. It is astonishing the irresistible attraction movable objects have for horses; like children, they love to play with things they can "jiggle about" themselves, and the more irritating and monotonous the resulting noise, it seems, the better they like it.

Careful consideration must be given to the flooring and drainage. In deciding the material to be employed, remember that a non-absorbent, hard floor offering good foot-hold is required. The old-fashioned cobble-stoned floor was as bad as the flag-paved one; the former permitted of no efficient drainage and the latter became dangerously slippery. Asphalt, of course, can be dismissed at once for the same reason. Since such types as grooved Blue Staffordshire bricks, which are ideal for the purpose, are rather costly, we are left with the most common, and possibly the cheapest, concrete. Concrete floors must be of sufficient thickness and strength to avoid cracking and breaking up, laid on about 9 inches of rubble, firmly rammed, and with only just enough gentle "fall" or slope to allow drainage (one in forty is sufficient). The finish should not be perfectly smooth, and to improve foot-hold and drainage it is advisable to groove the surface, the "herring-bone" pattern being found most suitable. This can be done by drawing a pointed stick along the concrete before it completely dries. The floor, of whatever material, should be higher than the level of the ground or yard outside for the sake of dryness.

Fittings. Fittings, such as manger, hay-rack, etc., inside the stable, are best kept to a minimum. Floor space is usually too valuable to be wasted, and the less the number of projections, the less the liability of injury. Wooden mangers are insanitary, being difficult to keep perfectly clean, and the old type of hay rack was usually placed at an inconvenient height which allowed seeds and dust to fall into the horse's eyes. Recently there was a craze for floor mangers, which had obvious objections from the point of view of cleanliness. It is quite possible to manage very well with no fittings at all; an exception can be made, on the grounds of convenience, in the case of a bridle-hook and this need only be a small thing of coat-hook type as it is only required to take the bridle for a few minutes during saddling and unsaddling.

To serve as a manger, a heavy metal bin of bucket shape, about seven gallons water capacity, can be obtained easily. This is quickly removed and easily cleaned after use, and kept out of the stable until the next meal. For the hay rack, substitute a string hay-net—do not just throw loose hay on the floor, it is soon spread about, trampled and soiled. Hay nets, besides being cheap, have the distinct advantage that they can be filled at any convenient spare time and then simply tied up in the box. More is said about hay nets in Chapter 12.

A word here about salt-licks, blocks of iodised or plain salt fixed in metal holders for screwing to the wall. Although properly they, like hay nets, come under the chapter on Feeding, being stable fittings they can be mentioned now. At first glance it would appear that salt always available to the horse would be beneficial to health and an ally against boredom. However, it has been suggested that salt-licks encourage such vices as crib-biting, since licking may lead to gnawing and this is before long transferred to any available woodwork. Experience, with some horses, seems to support this theory. The answer to the question "Is it worth the risk, however slight?" seems to be: there are enough little troubles to contend with without adding to them unnecessarily. The same objection can be applied to the practice of leaving a block of salt in a manger. So it is recommended that you banish them, supplying the necessary salt by sprinkling it on the food instead. The amount is dealt with in Chapter 11.

Food Store. The Food Store is an important part of the establishment, and one upon which some care and thought should be spent.

It is imperative that this building should be dry and provide as much protection as possible against vermin, dogs and unauthorised persons. It is not easy to make a forage barn completely vermin-proof and you will soon learn that a cat is no mere mascot in stables. Here a digression from horses may be excused; do remember that even a stable cat needs food and drink, a hungry one does not necessarily make the best ratter.

The position of the barn or food store is worth consideration. In old-fashioned stables it was the custom to build the hay-loft over the boxes or stalls, and a more inconvenient arrangement is difficult to imagine, as you will agree if you have ever been called upon to perform the necessary feats of strength and acrobatics in hauling a ton of hay up to a loft in 80 or 90 lb. bales, later running up and down a usually rickety and highly dangerous ladder every feeding time. This may be grand exercise but occasionally leads to loss of temper and the use of deplorable language. The best place for storing food is in a ground-floor building close to the stables, a spare loose-box being ideal for small quantities.

A large stock of food is economical and convenient, but only if it can be properly stored. This applies particularly to hay. Concrete floors can never be perfectly dry, and bales should be raised off them on bricks or lengths of timber to allow the air to circulate freely. As a guide to the size of the building, one ton of baled hay, that is, about 40 bales, takes approximately 84 cubic feet of space. Rat-proof corn bins should be provided for other food, such as oats, bran, etc., and even chaff if possible, since vermin cause considerable loss—more from tainting than by what they eat.

5

Stable routine, exercise and work

Daily Routine. With all animals, and possibly most of all with horses, a definite, regular routine is necessary. It is impossible to lay down hard and fast rules; circumstances have to be considered, but commonsense and thought for the animal's well-being and comfort are the foundation of such a routine.

The system must be built around a framework based on the recognition of certain facts. Feeds should be small, regular and frequent, and ample time allowed for their digestion. Suppose, then, that having decided to feed four times a day, which is recommended as a minimum number, the following approximate feeding times are arrived at: 8 a.m., midday, 4 p.m. and 8 p.m. Stablework and exercise will have to be fitted in with these times. It will be found in practice that 8 a.m. is rather late to begin the day's work, and 6.30 a.m. (or slightly later in winter) will be better. This means adding an extra meal, which is all to the good, but this need only be a small one—or an armful of hay. A routine can now be drawn up as follows:—

6.30 a.m.	Refill water buckets; give a small armful of hay; muck-out; quarter (see "Grooming" page 40).
7.30 a.m.	Feed.
9 to 11 a.m.	Remove droppings; exercise.
11.0 a.m.	Check water bucket; give a small armful of hay while washing and putting away tack; groom.
12.0 noon.	Remove droppings; feed.
2.0 p.m.	Clean stable and bed down. Give a small armful of hay and leave the horse to rest.
4.0 p.m.	Pick up droppings; quarter; exercise.
5.30 p.m.	Wisp (see "Grooming" page 44); straighten bedding; feed.

8.30 p.m. Pick up droppings; check water; straighten bedding; in winter adjust rugs; feed. (The final hay may be given now or later, say 10.0 p.m.)

In winter the routine can start half an hour later, and the afternoon exercise about 2.0 p.m. All these are approximate times and intended merely as a guide in arranging the daily programme.

The "Spare-Time" Owner. It is obvious that the previous timetable may be impossible for the "spare-time" horse keeper without a groom, and such an owner will have to adopt one of the systems suggested in Chapter 15, "Keeping Horses at Grass", since the animal cannot be kept standing in the stable all day. Hay nets, recommended in Chapter 12, will be invaluable in winter, and it should be possible to persuade a friend to feed the horse at least once during the day (do not expect him to fast during your absence)—another hay net can be left ready filled for your assistant to tie up.

Exercise and Work. As a general rule, a horse in condition requires at least two hours' exercise daily, and for a working animal adequate rest is essential. It will have been noticed, in the suggested programme, that a period of two hours was set aside for the horse to lie down and rest. During this time there should be quiet in the stable and no one should be allowed near the box. This was strictly enforced in cavalry stables, and is in well-run establishments, with the result that the horses were kept at the top of their condition and ready for anything. It is a practice that can be recommended to all busy riding stables.

The greater part of the exercise should be carried out at a walking pace, trotting for only about a quarter of the time. Hard work must not be demanded of a horse in soft condition, whether under saddle or in harness; he must be brought into full work gradually. Working a tired or unfit animal is a source of accidents and illness.

A really fit, properly fed horse is not easily overworked, provided certain conditions are observed. He must be considerately and intelligently ridden or driven, with a weight that is not too heavy and at a pace that is not too fast. Trotting should not exceed eight or nine miles per hour, and it should be realised that at the trot the forelegs suffer greater concussion when going downhill. In the case of riding horses, full use should be made of turf and other "soft going", avoiding cantering or galloping on hard ground. The legs can also be saved considerable strain by changing diagonals at the trot, that is, bumping once in the saddle and rising as the other foreleg comes to the ground. Draught horses should be relieved of the weight of their load when stopping on a hill, by the use of a block or a large stone placed behind a back wheel; remember to remove the stone or brick used for this purpose when the journey is resumed.

Long Rides. An experienced and considerate rider will follow the recognised old cavalry routine, saving his mount at every opportunity by dismounting when standing still, and halting for about a quarter of an hour every two or three hours, unsaddling and restoring circulation to the horse's back by massage or hand-slapping. Occasionally walking and leading with slackened girths for about half a mile relieves both horse and rider and can be done with greatest advantage on steep hills.

Whatever the length of the journey, girths should be checked after the first mile. They will often be found to have slackened by this time, or, rather, the horse will have resumed his normal dimension in this part if he is one which blows himself out at saddling time.

Leading on Foot. Ordinary common sense advises you never to ride a bicycle when leading a horse. Little control is possible from a bicycle, and you are recommended to take this advice.

On foot, you may lead a horse in a halter, headcollar or bridle, but even with the most reliable animal it is advisable to use a bridle when any distance is to be covered by road. With a double bridle, knot the bit, or curb, reins loosely and let them lie on the neck; pass the bridoon, or snaffle, reins over the horse's head, or unbuckle and take the off-rein through the near-side snaffle ring. A difficult horse may be easier to control when led by the bit reins. Whichever method is adopted, walk level with and close to the head, holding the reins or rope in the right hand, close to the bit, firmly but not so tightly as to interfere with the natural movement of the head; the ends of the reins or rope should be held in the left hand, but never twisted round it —which would allow little "give and take" when needed and can be dangerous. A useful tip, when the horse plays up, is to press the right forearm firmly against his neck, at the same time tensing the wrist, in which way more control is possible.

Leading when Riding. When riding one horse and leading another, both should be bridled, and it will usually be found better to lead by the bit reins as control is more difficult than when on foot. The length of the lead reins should be such as to keep both horses level and close together. Whether the reins of the led animal are held separately in the right hand, or whether they are taken in the bridle-hand with the others, is a matter for the individual to decide according to preference and the nature of the horses. If the led horse becomes troublesome and tries to break away, give to him at first by allowing his reins to slip through the fingers a little, then gradually bring him back to hand. In this way a "fight" is avoided and there is less danger of the reins being suddenly jerked from the hand, or the rider from the saddle. On no account, however quiet both horses may be, loop the lead reins over one finger—a sudden fright and a sharp tug may break it.

The rule of the road: The Highway code says that if you are riding a horse, you should keep to the left. And if you are leading a horse while riding another, you should still keep to the left, and keep the led animal on the left.

However, if you are on foot, and leading a horse, on a road that has no footpath, you should walk on the right-hand side of the road. You should walk between the horse and the traffic, and keep it as close as possible to the side of the road.

The Highway code does not say what to do on a road with a footpath, but usually in these "urban" areas a led horse will keep to the left. Local customs vary.

At all times the horseman is expected to use his judgement to avoid accidents, and occasionally this might necessitate taking a horse to the opposite side of the road from usual. Responsibility would rest with the horseman if an accident was caused through failure to do this. After sunset carry lights.

A horse-drawn vehicle, like any other vehicle, should always keep well in to the left.

It is illegal to drive, ride or lead a horse on any footpath or other way reserved for pedstrians at the side of the road. That it is sometimes necessary to break this law is not surprising under modern conditions.

We horsemen still have certain rights as road users, and it is well to know these:

Motorists are expected to slow down or stop if asked or signalled to do so by any person in charge of horses. When they do, please remember to acknowledge the courtesy.

It is the law that a motorist concerned in an accident causing injury to a "domestic animal" (this term legally includes all farm animals and dogs, but, for some unexplained reason, excludes poultry and cats) must stop and, on request, give the number of his vehicle, his own name and address and those of the owner of the vehicle. If he does not do this at the time, he is required to report the accident to a Police Station or Constable within 24 hours.

Broadly speaking, the rules of the road are a matter of commonsense, combined with consideration for others, and if they were observed by all, with a little courtesy added, our roads would be pleasanter to travel.

Entraining, etc. The problem of getting a horse into a horse-box, whether road or rail, is occasionally difficult, often leading to considerable excitement, loss of temper and accidents. In the majority of cases there would be less trouble if the task were tackled quietly and as a perfectly normal procedure, horses being quick to sense "an atmosphere". The ramp of the horse-box must be lowered and everything ready before the horse is brought to it, otherwise the unusual sights and sounds are certain to arouse misgivings in his mind. Take the further precaution of spreading a small quantity of straw over the ramp to reassure the animal with something familiar under his feet. The ramps of horse-boxes are provided with slats for foothold, but if necessary, ashes can be scattered on them for additional safety. If he is now led straight in without fuss as though into his own loose-box, there will probably be no resistance.

Unfortunately, the operation is not always so simple, however tactfully one approaches it, and one has to resort to guile or even force. When two horses are to be boxed, one that is known to be quiet should be led in first and the other may follow with confidence. If this fails, his stomach may over-rule his scruples if a feed or a hay-net are enticingly indicated inside the box. Even this does not always succeed, and one must prepare for trouble. If sending him by rail, guard against his getting a leg down between the

QUICK-RELEASE TETHERING KNOT

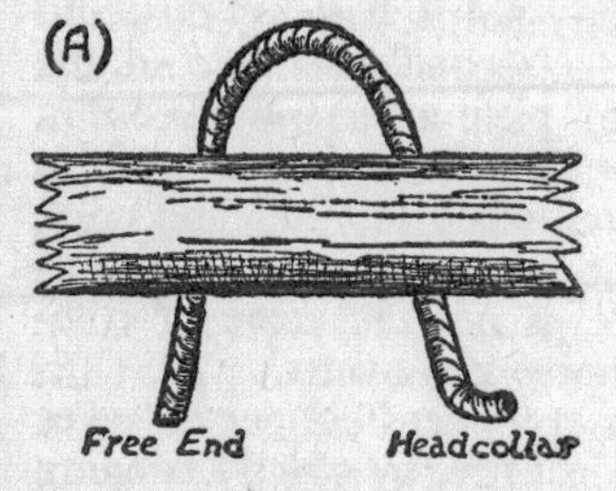

(A)
Make a loop behind the tethering bar or ring, short (free) end of rope on the left.

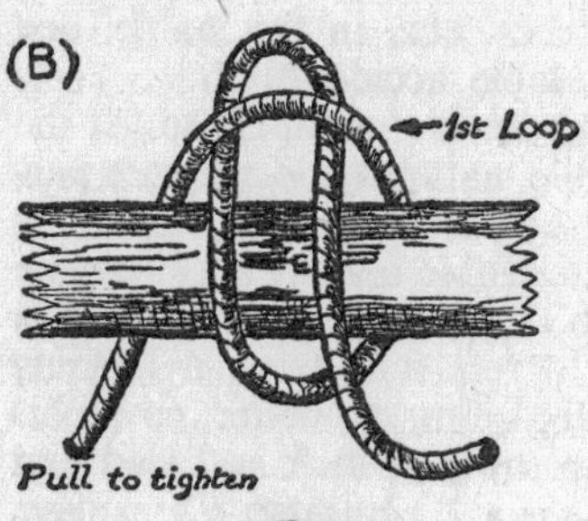

(B)
Make a loop on the headcollar side and pass through the first loop; pull the free end to tighten.

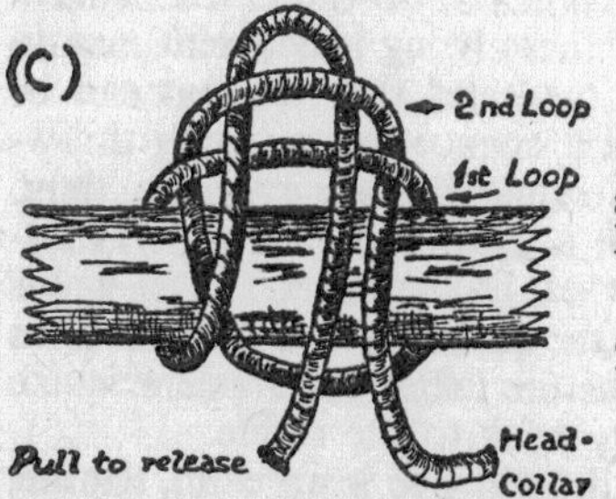

(C)
Make a loop in the free end and pass through the second loop; pull the headcollar end to tighten.

To release: Pull the free end sharply.

box and the platform in the excitement, by placing bales or sacks of straw either side of the entrance. He may now back in quite happily, or he may go in peacefully if blindfolded. Another way is to link hands behind the gaskins, with a second person, and pull him forward while a third leads by the headcollar. These latter methods should not be adopted until all other efforts have failed, as they are sure to excite and alarm him.

Be sure that he is watered before boxing, and satisfy yourself that he will be watered again at intervals during a long journey. Do not forget to provide him with food if he will be travelling for long; a hay net is best for this, and it may be necessary to have a second available in the groom's compartment. Hay to pick at usually keeps a horse quiet and happy. If possible, let someone familiar travel with him, especially by rail when shunting and noise can be very alarming. A long journey in the groom's compartment, especially over-night, is not the acme of comfort but is reassuring to both horse and owner.

Fire in the Stable. Although every sensible person takes all possible steps to guard against fire, by strictly banning smoking, the striking of matches, etc., in the stable, one must be prepared for unavoidable accidents.

In the event of an outbreak, the first action is to get the horses out as quickly as possible, naturally. Horses are particularly terrified of fire and quickly lose their heads, so that even the normally quiet, sensible animal may become stupid and difficult to handle. Although so terrified, it is not uncommon for a horse to refuse to leave a burning stable. If this happens, blindfold him, or, better, cover his eyes and nostrils with a damp towel or sack and lead him out. Try backing him out if he is still obstinate. Cases have occurred, in large stables, of there being insufficient men to deal with the number of horses, and then all that can be done is to give every animal a chance to escape by throwing open the doors, concentrating the attention on those that refuse to leave. In such a case, waste no time in undoing head-ropes of tied horses, unless quick-release knots have been used, simply cut the ropes and set them free as quickly as possible. Care must be taken that, once rescued, a horse does not break away back to the stable.

Now is the time, above all others, to keep calm, dealing quickly and efficiently but *quietly* with the task on hand. If there is any losing of heads to be done, the horses may be relied upon for this.

6
Bedding

HORSES are bedded down, primarily, to encourage them to lie down and rest. They can rest standing and, of course, there are horses which seldom lie down, but their condition is improved and the life of their legs increased by taking proper rest.

Inadequate bedding is almost as bad as none and is certainly false economy. A thin bed is quickly scraped away in places leaving the bare, hard floor exposed, from contact with which the elbows, fetlock joints and other parts are liable to injury, giving rise to such things as capped hock and capped elbow. Also there will be an unnecessarily wet and dirty horse to be groomed in the morning.

There are various materials which may be used for bedding, straw (of which there are several kinds) and peat moss being the most usual; others, which will be briefly considered but which are by no means as satisfactory, are: sawdust and shavings, sand, leaves and bracken. Hay, naturally, is not used, except possibly when musty or otherwise unpalatable, but this is unsatisfactory as, apart from being eaten by greedy horses, it very quickly becomes a heavy, sodden mass.

Of the varieties of straw, wheat is recognised as the best, being long and harder than the others and providing better drainage through its tubes. Oat straw is more readily eaten and, not being so hard as wheat straw is more easily flattened, with consequent loss of drainage properties. Barley straw is unsuitable, being a soft straw which is very quickly flattened, and unless an unusually large amount is used soon becomes a thin, hard bed. A further drawback is that the awns of barley straw may give rise to eye trouble, or if eaten may cause colic. Rye straw would make a very excellent litter if it were obtainable.

With all varieties of straw, the modern practice of baling is a great disadvantage as the compression in a bale crushes the straws considerably, rendering them less capable of good drainage. Quite frequently, on opening a bale of straw, one finds a mass of useless chaff. For these reasons, try to have trussed straw, which, if it does take up more storage space, is less wasteful. If buying in the stack, the weight can be estimated at 16 cubic yards to the ton.

Peat moss is used considerably as bedding, being particularly useful for horses that will eat straw, but it must be emphasised at once that unless properly laid and looked after, it becomes a menace to the horse that is kept on it. It is often allowed to become filthy and leads to foot trouble.

The other materials can be quite briefly dealt with:

Sawdust calls for even greater attention than peat moss, and the whole bed must be well turned every day. It quickly becomes heated when damp, and again foot trouble follows.

Shavings, of course, are not very absorbent but do not heat so quickly as sawdust. Apart from the fact that large chips of wood may be found in them, shavings are at the best a poor substitute.

Sand does make quite a good bed in warm, dry weather and is therefore not popular in Great Britain. Should it by any mischance be eaten in any quantity, as it may if it contains salt, sand colic will result.

Leaves and bracken, unless nothing else offers, can be dismissed as unsuitable, being capable neither of absorbing moisture nor draining it off.

Bedding down with Straw. Your aim in bedding down with straw will be to provide a warm, level, elastic yet firm bed which will drain away moisture, provide protection against floor draughts and prevent injury from hard surfaces. If these points are remembered you will not go wrong.

Shake out the straw thoroughly when laying it, and, starting from the edges of the box, toss it so that it lies evenly over the floor with the straws crossing in different directions. If it is thrown down in lumps and with the straws lying parallel it is less elastic and is soon dragged around by the horse's feet, leaving bare or thin patches, Push the bed well up against the sides and back of the box to give a saucer effect, which will be protection against draughts or injury from the walls. At the front, by the door, leave a bare space if the floor is above the level of the ground outside, as it should be. This "doorstep" avoids an untidy appearance and is a "mind the step" notice to the horse when going in or out of the box. Finish the edge off by turning the straggling edges under neatly.

When using old and new bedding together, mix the two well before bedding down. Remember a good thick bed is an economy; apart from the comfort of the horse there will be less wastage and it will be so much easier to muck-out in the morning.

A common trouble with all types of straw, even wheat, is that of its being eaten by the horse. Many and varied are the remedies suggested—some say it is because the horse does not get sufficient hay, others advise tying him up as though he were in a stall—but still many horses turn to their bedding as an extra course. From experience, sprinkling the bed with Jeyes, or some other safe disinfectant, has usually been found effective in checking the habit. Time will show how much must be sprinkled. With animals which, however, look upon a dash of disinfectant as a condiment, I have found spraying the bed with "Flit", "Cooper McDougall's" or a similar fly-spray provides the answer.

Bedding down with Peat Moss. Firstly. the entrance to the drains having been stopped up to prevent their becoming blocked, the peat must be laid at least eight inches deep and well rolled so that it will not be constantly churned up as the horse moves about.

Secondly, it must receive constant attention—remember that this bed is always down, unlike straw which can be completely removed for part of the day. Droppings must be removed even more frequently than is often the case with straw litter. Wet patches, likewise, must be taken out regularly and the place covered either with fresh peat moss or clean sawdust; a point to note here is that sawdust alone heats quickly, but mixed with peat in this way is quite a safe bedding.

Lastly, even stricter attention must be paid to cleanliness of the horse's feet.

All these points are extremely important because peat moss is very absorbent and is a deodorizer, for which reasons dirty patches may easily be missed unless removed immediately, with consequent ill-effects on the condition of the feet. It will be appreciated at once that although it may be possible to keep an eye on the litter during the day (especially if one has a groom to take the blame for neglect) it is a different matter during the night, and it is not difficult to imagine the state of the bed in the morning, particularly with some horses. In any case, peat moss is inclined to stain light-coloured coats, with which one has enough trouble in the ordinary way.

Correctly managed, then, peat moss litter makes a very excellent, economical bedding, although not nearly so attractive in appearance as good wheat straw, but unless you are prepared to give it the attention it demands, avoid it.

Having said so much about this type of litter, it is only fair to point out that, like so many other things to-day, it is at times difficult to obtain and when available is only too often poor, dirty stuff and quite frequently already damp when delivered.

Mucking-out

"Mucking-out" is the very appropriate term applied to the early morning cleaning of the stables.

Having already mentioned the attention required by peat moss litter and similar forms of bedding, it only remains to deal with straw. The task is simple enough—the separation of the clean from the wet, dirty bedding and droppings—but requires some practice. Using the two-pronged "stable fork", the clean straw is removed first to a convenient corner and then, in the interests of economy, that which is not too wet or dirty to be used again is shaken from the remainder and follows the clean. Now the short and the dirty stuff, together with the droppings, are swept up, loaded on to a wheelbarrow and carted away to the manure heap. This heap adorns a corner of the premises not near enough to be unpleasant and not so far away as to necessitate a long journey; a brick enclosure is ideal for storing manure.

Soiled bedding which is to be re-used is best kept out of the box or stall altogether, so that the horse is not forced to breathe foul air, and the floor can air and dry thoroughly. In suitable weather it can be spread out in the open if space permits, and in wet weather in any open shed or spare loose-box.

Regularly and frequently the floor should be washed down with plenty of water plus disinfectant, special attention being given to the corners, and the drains sluiced out. While horses are out, keep all windows and doors wide open to air the place completely. In summer, spraying with a good proprietary fluid helps to keep down flies and other insects and makes the stable healthy and pleasant.

7

Grooming

To understand the reasons for grooming it is necessary to know something about the skin and the coat.

There are two skins, the moist, sensitive "dermis", containing the roots of the hair, the sweat and oil glands, bloodvessels and nerves; protecting the dermis is the dry, insensitive "epidermis", which is constantly being shed in the form of scurf. The purpose of sweating is to keep the body temperature level, and, through the pores, to throw off some of its waste products. The coat, providing warmth and protection, is greased and waterproofed by the oil glands.

In domestication, the horse works harder and faster, consuming more heat-producing foods than in its natural state, so that the skin and the sweat glands are called upon to function more actively. To enable them to carry out their work efficiently, the skin must be kept clean by grooming, and the sweat glands stimulated by massage. Cleanliness is also a preventive of skin diseases which are encouraged to spread by dirty conditions, whilst massage assists in toning up the muscles.

In attaining these objects, the final purpose of grooming is automatically achieved—appearance.

Grooming Kit

There are certain tools used for the various operations of grooming:—

Hoof Pick. The hoof pick is a blunt iron hook used for removing dirt and stones from the feet. When used it is not forced down the side or cleft of the frog harder than necessary, and is worked from the heel to the toe.

Dandy Brush. The dandy brush is usually of stiff whisk fibre and is employed for the removal of hard, caked dirt from the coat, particularly on the legs.

Body Brush and Curry Comb. These are always used together. The brush, of short, stout bristles, with a loop of webbing across the back to keep it on the hand, is for removing scurf and dirt. There are two types of Curry Comb, the handiest being the Cavalry pattern, which consists of a metal plate with several blunt-toothed blades on one side and a webbing loop on the other for securing it to the *back* of the hand. The other type is the "Jockey", which is fitted with a wooden handle instead of the hand loop. The advantage of the first is that the palm of the hand on which it is secured is left free and can be placed on the horse during grooming. The purpose of the curry comb is primarily for cleaning the body brush of collected scurf; an occasional rub is given on the brush and the side of the comb is knocked on the floor. It is, however, effective used on the horse for the removal of dried mud with which the dandy brush is unable to deal.

Water Brush. The water brush is a very gentle one, with softer and longer bristles than the others, and in addition to its purpose of damping the mane and tail, and washing the legs and feet (when really necessary), is excellent for grooming the head and face which are too sensitive for stiffer brushes.

Sponge and Stable Rubber. For cleaning the eyes, lips, nostrils and dock, a sponge is generally used, but a damp rubber, or stable cloth, is often preferred as a substitute. The intended use of the rubber is for giving the coat a final polish after grooming.

Mane and Tail Comb. This is, or should be, rarely needed. It is made of horn, or more commonly these days, light metal, and has broad teeth. This comb should be used as little as possible in actual grooming as it is very liable to do more harm than good, by breaking or tearing out the hair. It may be found necessary in such operations as plaiting the mane, "pulling" the mane and tail, or trimming leg feathering, all of which are described in Chapter 8.

Sweat Scraper. This is a long, flexible metal strip or blade with a handle at either end, and is used for scraping the lather from a sweating horse, as the name suggests. It is, however, far better that your horse should not be allowed to get into such a state that a sweat scraper is required.

Wisp. This is possibly the most useful tool of all, and, strange to say, the cheapest. It is a twisted rope of hay or straw about eight feet long, with two loops at one end, the rope being plaited around each loop in turn and secured at the end in one of the twists.

Method of Grooming

Perhaps the best way of describing the method of grooming will be to deal with it as it occurs in the daily routine.

Quartering. Before exercising it is desirable to "quarter" —known in the stables as "knocking over"—which is merely a quick, light grooming to make the horse presentable. In this, as in all grooming operations, start by picking out the feet, as already described. Follow this by brushing off all stable marks with the dandy; if the horse has been properly bedded down the previous evening, these marks will be few and dry. Then, with the body brush, quickly brush down the mane and tail. The head and face can be rubbed over, and the eyes, nose, lips and dock sponged. The whole operation should take only five or ten minutes.

Cooling and Drying. On returning from exercise or work the horse should, ordinarily, be cool and dry but if he is wet or sweating he must be dried immediately. In any case it is advisable to leave the saddle on for a few minutes as a chill preventative—undo the girths, ease the saddle from the back and then girth up again loosely. When the saddle is finally taken off, the back must either be dried at once or else covered until it has cooled. If the horse has been at work for some time, the circulation of the blood in the back will have been somewhat interfered with by pressure and weight and should be restored by vigorous slapping with the hands.

When wet from rain, wisping with loose straw followed by the rubber, will get the horse dry and warm. The heels and the backs of the pasterns will also need to be dried to prevent greasy heels, the best way being with a handful of clean sawdust. Bran was at one time used for this purpose, and perhaps one day it will be again. The feel of the ears is an indication of the warmth of the body, so work on your horse until they are normally warm. "Ear stripping", as it is called, is carried out by standing in front of the horse and gently pulling an ear through each hand to dry or warm it; most horses love it.

Breaking-out. It sometimes happens, usually with an animal out of condition, that breaking-out is met with, that

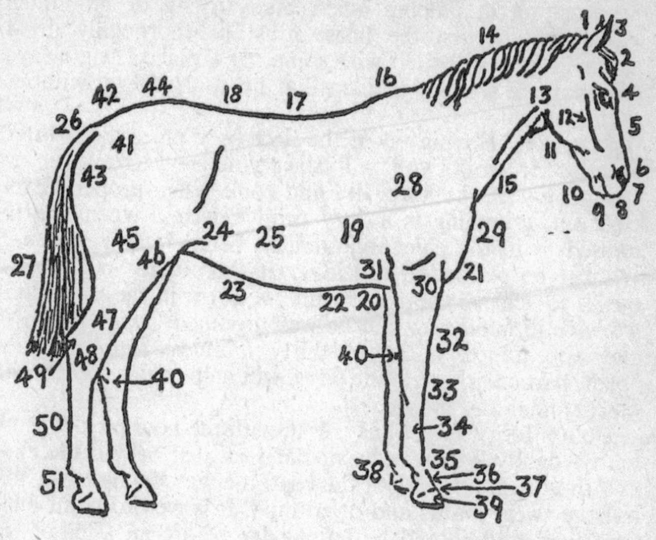

KEY TO POINTS OF THE HORSE

Head and Neck

1. Poll (Nape of Neck)
2. Forelock
3. Ears
4. Forehead
5. Face
6. Muzzle
7. Nostrils
8. Upper Lip
9. Lower Lip
10. Chin Groove
11. Lower Jaw
12. Cheekbone
13. Jowl
14. Mane (Crest)
15. Throat (Windpipe)

Trunk or Body

16. Withers
17. Back
18. Loins
19. Side of Chest
20. Girth Place
21. Breast (Chest)
22. Floor of Chest
23. Belly
24. Flank
25. Barrel

Tail

26. Dock (Root of Tail)
27. Hair of Tail

Limbs and Croup

28. Shoulder
29. Point of Shoulder
30. Arm (True Arm)
31. Elbow
32. Forearm
33. Knee
34. Cannon (Shank) Bone
35. Fetlock Joint
36. Pastern
37. Coronet
38. Heels
39. Hoof
40. Chestnut
41. Haunch
42. Croup
43. Hip Joint
44. Point of Hip
45. Upper Thigh
46. Stifle
47. Lower Thigh
48. Hock
49. Point of Hock
50. Flexor Tendons
51. Feathering

is, sweating in patches again after drying or grooming. When this occurs, the horse must be thoroughly dried again, or he may be left with some straw placed lengthways on the back under a rug, so that he cools slowly without taking a chill.

Strapping. Having taken the necessary precautions after exercise or work, you will start your real grooming or strapping with the horse dry and cool. When properly carried out, grooming is a very tiring business when one is unused to it, the chief requirement being "elbow grease". It must be performed quickly, yet thoroughly and vigorously, to achieve the best results; a horse in the condition we have in mind now can be well groomed, for cleanliness and appearance, in about thirty minutes. Further time spent, particularly with the wisp, will help to put muscle on both animal and groom.

Do not forget to get busy, first, with the hoof pick. Then, with a dandy brush, begin at the neck just behind the ear and thoroughly brush out the coat, the way the hair lies, to remove sweat marks and dried mud. It is well to point out here that mud should be left to dry before an attempt is made to brush it off. If preferred, it may be washed off before it dries, but if this is done the skin must be thoroughly dried afterwards with sawdust, straw, etc., or chapping of the skin will result.

It is often asked why this careful drying should be necessary, since horses can be kept out all the year round or can work in the rain without ill effects. The answer is that the natural waterproof greasiness of the coat is not removed in these cases, and in the latter instance the circulation is maintained by movement. However, cracked (chapped) heels *are* occasionally found in horses at grass.

After the dandy brush comes the real work with the body brush, getting right through the coat and clearing scurf and dried sweat from the skin itself. It is customary to begin on the near side, that is, the horse's left, when for the most part the brush will be on the left hand and the curry comb on the right; on the offside the brush will be on the right hand and the curry comb on the left. In this way more force can be used behind the brush. Take your stand, with the feet apart, a little away from the horse so that weight can be put on the brush to drive the bristles through the coat, steadying yourself with the right hand on the horse—and here is the advantage of the cavalry type of curry comb, leaving the palm of the hand free. Remember to scrape the body brush across the curry comb periodically during grooming, to remove scurf and dust, but do not put more work into cleaning the brush than you do into cleaning the horse. With a vigorous circular motion, work down the neck and along the body, not forgetting the part between the forelegs and the belly, finishing by using the brush in the direction of the coat. Now turn your attention to the near legs, not neglecting the inside of the thighs. When grooming the hindlegs, particularly on the inside, grasp the hamstring with the free hand; it may be a ticklish spot you are dealing with now and the hold on the hamstring is a guard against kicks. Many grooms prefer to brush the inside of the opposite legs while on the near side and do the inside of the near legs when working on the off-side. Now repeat the whole process on the other side.

By this time, if you have been grooming properly, you should feel as if you had been doing some hard work. However, the next item is one which must be dealt with gently. For the head it is much better to use the water brush, even the body brush may be too severe for this sensitive part. Do not forget the ears, brush them out against the palm of the hand, the tip of the ear held under the thumb.

The mane comes next, and here you should use the body brush, as the dandy is inclined to pull and break the hair. Here, as elsewhere, scurf must be removed from the *roots*. First brush the mane out to clear any tangles—do not use the mane comb for this purpose unless the mane is very thick. Then brush out lock by lock for cleanliness and finally straight down. A well-kept mane enhances a horse's appearance.

Now clean the eyes, nostrils, lips and dock, in that order, with a damp sponge or cloth. Wash out the sponge or cloth thoroughly afterwards.

The tail should be dealt with in a similar fashion to the mane. The subject of tail-pulling and bandaging is discussed in the Chapters "Clipping and Trimming" and "Clothing", but all that is necessary now is to get the hair clean and lying down smoothly. A damp water brush will help to make the hair at the root tidy.

To put the finishing touches to the grooming operations,

give the coat a final polish with the stable rubber—a chamois leather is excellent for this.

Your horse should now be clean and smart, but, unless time is limited, before using the rubber put in some work with the wisp. This is slapped down smartly on the coat in the direction of the hair but is not used on the head, loins, or any delicate sensitive parts. A quick wisping again in the evening is beneficial.

Washing. Washing horses is not a common practice in England, for obvious reasons, although in warm climates it can safely be carried out. In this country, washing should be limited to removing stains from grey or other light-coloured horses, and to the mane and tail when necessary. The sheath, or penis, in geldings must be washed out occasionally, and the feet may be after picking out. It is, in fact, a wise precaution to wash out the feet now and then, adding a few drops of Jeyes' Fluid to the water, and may help to avoid "thrush", which is a smelly discharge from the cleft of the frog caused by dirty conditions. White socks, stockings, etc., often have to be washed for appearance (it may be from this that the legend of the weakness of white legs has grown), but they must be *thoroughly* dried afterwards. It is doubtful whether such washing is always necessary; on most occasions just as good results can be obtained by ample use of the body brush.

8
Clipping and trimming

Reasons for Clipping. In winter, the horse grows a thicker and longer coat for protection and as some compensation for the decreased quality and quantity of food available in natural conditions. Under domestication, the necessary food is supplied (or should be) by man, but protection against cold is still required and nature continues to provide the winter coat, which makes its appearance in the autumn and is shed again in the spring.

For a horse living out at grass, the extra covering, and its additional grease, are essential. Taking no more exercise than necessary, or than he feels inclined to, no body heat is lost, nor discomfort suffered, from sweating. For a stabled and working animal, however, a thick coat has many disadvantages. None of us would care to perform hard physical work while dressed in a fur coat; we would perspire freely and tire quickly. So it is with a horse; he cannot be expected to work thus and keep condition. Satisfactory grooming is difficult, with the result that the pores become clogged with waste products which cannot be properly cleared from the skin. Drying after work, and possibly a soaking with rain or snow, is even more difficult and laborious, and chills follow. All these troubles are overcome by clipping.

When not working, a clipped horse must be compensated for the loss of his coat by clothing, or chills again are invited. Clothing takes the form of "rugs", varying in number according to the temperature. Types of clothing are dealt with in Chapter 9.

Times for Clipping. In a normal year, the winter coat is usually well-established in October or November, and the first clipping can take place then, followed by a second early in the new year. The theory that clipping after the new year spoils the summer coat is unfounded, and although twice is sometimes sufficient, the clippers may be used whenever the hair grows noticeably. Directly the summer coat shows signs of coming through in the spring (probably April or May) there should be no more clipping, but it is seldom that it need continue far into the year. The coat reacts quickly to changes in temperature, and the dates for first and last clipping can only be decided by weather conditions.

Types of Clip. There are three types of clip to suit different purposes:—

For a draught horse, working only at slow paces, the "trace-high" method is used. Only the belly and upper parts of the legs are clipped, that is, from the middle of the forearms and gaskins to approximately the trace height of cart harness, level with the points of the shoulders. The mane and tail, of course, are left.

For a saddle horse or a light draught horse, doing fairly fast work, it is usual to clip "right out" or "down to the ground". As the terms indicate, the whole body, legs and head, are clipped, leaving only the tail, mane and forelock—unless the mane is already "hogged", that is clipped short.

The "Hunter's Clip" is a variation of the last, the difference being that the legs are only partly clipped, as in trace-high, but sometimes a "saddle-patch" is left on the back by clipping around the saddle. It is a common practice to clip "right-out" the first time and to adopt the Hunter's Clip subsequently in the year, especially for fine-coated animals.

As there is controversy as to the merits of the Hunter's Clip, the arguments for and against are set out below:—

For leaving the legs:

(*a*) Protection from cold and from thorns, etc.

(*b*) The hair on the back of the fetlock joints acts as a drain for sweat and wet, preventing cracked heels (chapping) by keeping them dry.

Against:

(*a*) It does not afford *complete* protection from thorns, and when these are picked up they are more easily detected and removed without the hindrance of long hair.

(*b*) There is little force in the "dain" reasoning, since unclipped horses at grass sometimes suffer from cracked heels, and in a stabled horse, the legs, clipped or not, must be dried on return from work if they are wet, the task being more difficult with long, thick hair; in any case a small tuft could be left at the back of the joint to act as a drain.

For a saddle-patch:

(*a*) Saddle galls are prevented.

(*b*) Short hairs left after complete clipping may be a source of irritation if forced into the back by the rider's weight.

(*c*) A cold saddle on a clipped back is disliked and may cause bucking.

Against:

(*a*) How can the coat prevent galling, since saddle injuries are caused by friction due to loose girthing or bad riding, or by pressure from an ill-fitting saddle on parts unprotected by muscle?

(*b*) The point about irritation from short "stump" hairs, reasonable in theory, is unsupported in practice—at least to any appreciable extent.

(*c*) The objection to a cold saddle can be overcome by saddling up loosely a few minutes before mounting, as should always be done with any horse.

(*d*) A saddle patch causes considerable sweating of the back and there is danger of chills if it is not properly dried; drying the back is extra work avoided by clipping.

From these arguments the reader will conclude there is little or no advantage in the Hunter Clip or saddle patch.

Types of Machines. There are two kinds of clippers, hand and power, both resembling the hair-dresser's implements. The first, almost identical with the old manual hair-dressing instrument, with two small handles, is suitable only for hogging manes, trimming fetlocks, etc. The second is subdivided into the hand-power (or "wheel") machine and the electrically-operated. For hand-power clippers a second person is needed to turn the wheel, which is mounted on a stand and, by gears, supplies power through a flexible cable to the knives, or blades. In the electrically-operated machine, like the modern hair-dresser's, the vibrating motor is normally in the hand-grip, power being supplied through a flex or cable plugged into a convenient electric point.

The Operation. Choose a mild day for clipping; a cold, blustery spell is no time for depriving the horse of his natural overcoat, and, of course, do not clip if he has a cold or is in any other way "off colour". Even though you will be rugging up afterwards, he needs a little time to become acclimatised. Be sure everything is in order for going straight through with operations without any hitch; the clippers must be sharp, blunt knives mean hard work and indifferent results, and there must be sufficient time to finish the job without a last-minute rush. Have the horse thoroughly clean or the clippers will soon be blunted.

If you are using a wheel machine, try to obtain an assistant who can be relied upon to work at a steady rate and who is not likely to tire before you have finished—turning is not as easy as it may seem. It may be necessary to have a third person available if your horse is liable to play-up; some will stand quietly, tied or loose, while others may even need the "twitch". (A twitch distracts the horse's attention from an unpleasant operation by inflicting pain on the nose and upper lip—the most sensitive parts; it consists of a round stick—like a broomstick or stable-fork handle—about 18 inches or 2 feet long, with a piece of rope threaded through a hole in the end. The rope is formed into a loop large enough to admit the fist, placed on the upper lip and the tip of the nose, and the stick given a turn or two. It should never be used brutally, should be kept on for no longer than necessary, and the nose should be gently massaged afterwards to restore circulation. *Avoid it whenever possible.*)

If in doubt at first, begin by treating him as perfectly quiet, only resorting to methods of restraint when absolutely necessary. Never use more drastic means than are warranted; gentle treatment quietens most animals, violence and the infliction of pain confirms fear. Lastly, have a dandy brush and some oil at hand, as you must frequently clear the blades of loose hair and lubricate them, afterwards cleaning off surplus oil that could be transferred to the coat.

The stand of a wheel machine should be placed at a safe distance from the horse, but not so far away as to hinder the clipper, and the cable should at all times run straight back from the knives, kinks and curves being avoided; to achieve this it will have to be moved several times during the work, and it is the turner's responsibility to anticipate any moves required as different parts are clipped. To keep the stand steady, he will find it best to place a foot firmly on one of the legs, and his free hand on the head of the stand.

Where you start on a horse is a matter of choice. Some begin at the neck, others prefer the hindquarters, but the head is usually left to the last. First get the knives moving steadily, then apply them to the coat against the lay of the hair, with an even pressure to avoid a ridgy effect. Very little practice is required to take the coat off evenly on the broader expanses, but at "corners" and the angle of bones some skill is called for; loose skin, such as at the junction of the elbows with the body, should be pulled flat. At the crest take care not to run up into the mane, edge the coat off gradually to leave a smooth finish—this is particularly necessary when the mane is not hogged. Where the tail joins the body, at the top, leave a small "V", pointing forward, to give a neat effect. In the head, the bones are near the surface and you must work with care—watch also the root of the forelock, do not go too far and cut the long hair. You will notice "feelers" or whiskers on the muzzle; many people take these off to save themselves trouble, but *they must be left*, and the skilful man clips carefully around them. The ears you can deal with easily by holding them *flat* in your free hand and running the blades downwards from their tips; do not clip inside, fold them together and run the clippers along the edges.

In "Trace-high" and "Hunter's Clip", slant the boundary line of the hair that is being left, upwards and forwards. For neatness, lightly trim the long feathering at the backs of the legs, edging off the hair around so that no obvious ridge is left. Should you have decided, also, to leave a saddle patch in the Hunter's Clip, your horse must be saddled up to mark the boundary; having clipped around the saddle to get the correct shape, take it off and cut your patch a little smaller so that it will not show when the horse is saddled.

Operations completed, brush the horse down and rug up immediately—in fact it is advisable to throw a rug over when the body is finished. For a few days after, increase the food ration slightly and allow more bedding to compensate for loss of warmth.

Trimming

Trimming can be defined as the process of making a horse's appearance smarter and neater and approximating more nearly to one with more "quality", by reducing the coarse hair and feathering. It includes, also, "tidying up" the mane and tail when these grow unevenly or straggly. Scissors and a comb are generally used in place of clippers, and long or unwanted hair is pulled out by hand. It is an art which calls for skill and practice, and great care must be exercised, especially in early attempts, or the result will be worse.

Legs. Long, coarse hair or feathering should be trimmed with scissors and comb, leaving them smooth and even. To achieve this, it is better to take your time and remove only a little at each cut—you cannot replace hair and it takes a long time to grow and cover mistakes.

Mane. On occasions the mane has to be "levelled", that is, the hair which grows down beyond the general length and gives it an untidy appearance, has to be pulled out—a few hairs only at a time.

It is rarely necessary to hog the mane, and it is good to note that this is less frequently done now. A few horses may look better without their manes, such as those which grow only a poor, short one, but often its removal discloses or accentuates a "ewe neck" which was better hidden. (A ewe neck is one shaped like a sheep's, curving downwards in the middle.) For hogging, hand clippers are used, care being taken not to leave a sharp dividing line where the hair of the neck is met.

Keeping the mane all on one side (custom says the off-side) is really a matter of grooming, when a damped water brush is usually sufficient to "lay" it. Stubborn manes, however, may be layed by plaiting, and for bad cases it may be necessary to purchase a special "mane-layer" to attach to the bottom of the mane. In the stable it obviously does not matter how many plaits you make, but when dressing-up for the show ring it is "not done" to have more than six. They should not be left in for more than a day at a time or there will be a tendency for the hair to break. When it is unplaited, brush out the mane well and get the curls out.

Tail. The clippers are never used on the tail. If it is

desired to level the end, use scissors or special tail shears. The length is largely a matter of taste, and from the horse's point of view, the longer the better, but many people like it shortened ("banged") to four or six inches above the points of the hocks when the horse is moving—at which time he lifts it slightly. Personally I consider this too short, but then I prefer a natural tail and do not object to the slight extra work of brushing out mud. To cut the tail, raise it to judge the required length, then, with a second person holding it with a hand either side of the place chosen, cut so that there is a very slight downward and backward slope, that is, the hair nearest the horse is a little shorter than on the outside.

"Pulling" the tail, or making it neat and tidy at the root, must be carried out a little at a time to avoid soreness, a few hairs from the lower part being removed at each pull, and any long hairs from the sides. Do not interfere with the hairs on the outer surface and never cut the tail near the root, or a bristly effect will result. This is frequently hard on the fingers, which may become cut in the process, so a mane comb can be used, the hair being twisted into the teeth. Tail-pulling is a fetish with many grooms (and others) and one often sees horses with tails almost naked half-way down the dock, but sensibly carried out it does make a great improvement in appearance. However, if you do not feel equal to the task, good grooming does much to keep a tail tidy, and your horse will be none the worse—probably far happier. Remember, too, a horse living out needs all the protection from weather that he can get, and which a bushy tail provides for the delicate parts beneath. In the horse world, even yet, there is too much care and thought bestowed on custom, tradition and appearance, and not enough on the animal itself (example: docking). Keep your horse fit and well by good feeding, grooming and general management and his appearance will be a source of pride without any beauty parlour treatment. To those who still maintain that a well-kept tail is the sign of a good groom, I can only retort (in a book)—"Nonsense".

9
Clothing

FOR all normal stable purposes, a day and a night rug are all that are necessary in the way of clothing for the clipped horse. In severe weather, two can be used at a time, or an ordinary blanket placed underneath one. For horses kept out all the year round, the two types of waterproof rugs described later in this chapter have been found invaluable for fine-coated animals or others who cannot stand up to the winter; although sometimes recommended for *clipped* horses living out, the wisdom of clipping horses that must winter out is doubtful.

Night Rug. This is made of jute, or similar material, bound at the edges with leather and lined with woollen blanketing. They are obtainable, also, in wool throughout, but these are more expensive and less easily cleaned; the advantage claimed for them is that they allow freer evaporation from a horse that is not thoroughly dry. The cheaper rug is more generally used and is found satisfactory.

It extends from the root of the tail to the withers, thence downward and forward around the base of the neck, meeting at the middle of the breast, and reaches down to the level of the elbows. Three stock sizes are usual: "Pony" (up to 14 h.h.), "Cob" (14 to 15 h.h.) and "Horse" or "Hunter" (above 15 h.h.). It is shaped to the contours of the body, that is, with allowance for the rise at the withers and quarters. There are variations in fastenings, some having a leather strap and a buckle at the breast, others having webbing pieces and cords for tying. To prevent the rug from slipping sideways, it may have a surcingle attached, that is, a broad webbing strap passing over the back, fastening on the near side either by buckles or strings. It is better, however, to have instead a separate "roller", a surcingle well padded where it crosses the spine, to obviate injury from pressure, and fitted with buckles and leather straps on the near side. With the former it is advisable to place a thick, soft pad under the surcingle either side of the backbone, so shaped that this part is free from direct or indirect pressure. At the hindquarters there may be one of two methods of securing; by a braided cord ("fillet string") passing round the buttocks from one rear corner of the rug to the other, or by a fillet string on either side, from further forward, passing inside each thigh to fasten at the rear edge of the rug. The purpose of fillet strings is to prevent the corners from blowing up or being otherwise displaced.

Day Rug. In size and design this is similar to the night rug, but is made of wool only (for winter use) and has no surcingle attached, a separate roller being employed. Where strict economy is essential, night rugs are often found serving also during daytime. Less restricted establishments sometimes use a thin, light rug of cotton ("summer" or "day sheet") for warm days, to keep the coat clean after grooming.

Waterproof Rugs. These outdoor rugs are made of waterproofed canvas, lined with blanketing, and are more loosely fitting at the lower ("skirt") part than stable rugs, to allow freedom of movement. They buckle at the breast, in the same way, but strong leather straps with spring hooks take the place of fillet strings. In the "New Zealand", these are the only fittings, but the "All Weather" rug has, in addition, a crupper or tail loop, and a surcingle, which, instead of encircling the rug completely, passes through a small opening on each side at the position of the horse's girth-place, so avoiding gathering of the rug at this part which would result in restriction of the forelegs. Both are made in the usual sizes, Pony, Cob and Hunter.

It is claimed for these rugs that they afford sufficient protection from the weather, and that they right themselves after rolling. There is no doubt they are useful, but particular care is necessary in their fitting, and they should be adjusted frequently. As all rugs tend to slide back and the withers and shoulders soon become chafed, it is a wise precaution to pad them here. In the New Zealand, since there is no surcingle, the leg straps have to be tight enough to keep it in place, and these must have frequent, generous treatment with neatsfoot oil, not only to preserve the leather but to keep it soft, the tender skin inside the thighs being especially liable to chafing. The surcingle on the All Weather rug must be inspected regularly to see that it has not tightened.

"Rugging-up." The right way to put on a rug is *not* to throw it on and then jiggle it straight. First fold it inside out, with the tail end up as far as the neck opening; then holding it at this part, the right hand taking the off, and the left the near side, gently throw it across the withers from the near side, further forward than it will be when fastened. Now buckle or tie at the breast and unfold the rug so that its centre line lies along the backbone; do not, even now, pull it back as far as it will go, leave the neck opening rather loose—in the way of all rugs it will slide back all too soon and tighten there. Before fastening the surcingle, make sure it lies flat; being out of sight, the off-side has a sneaky way of twisting, and it will usually manage a double twist so that nothing is suspected. With a roller, loosely fold up the longer end, place the pad in position immediately behind the withers, push the folded end down on the offside, then bring it under the horse at the girth place and buckle on the near side. With both surcingle and roller, straighten out any wrinkles in the skirt of the rug after fastening, and do not buckle uncomfortably tightly—you should be able to run the fingers down, flat, between it and the rug to straighten it. Finally tie the fillet strings—not tightly, but so that they hang in a loop reaching to just above halfway up the gaskins (except in the New Zealand).

Cleaning Rugs. When both day and night rugs are used, one can be aired while the other is worn. In all cases they should be shaken out and brushed on both sides when taken off. Night rugs are particularly liable to soiling and it may be necessary to scrub them lightly—with the minimum of water—stretching while drying, to avoid shrinking.

Clothing being an easy medium for the spread of contagious diseases, each horse should have his own rug which should not be used on any other even when apparently healthy.

BANDAGES

The practice of bandaging is still abused in many stables, and, as in many other matters, has become almost a convention with little regard to necessity. Whilst bandages are useful in certain circumstances, they can be harmful, especially when inexpertly applied; it is generally recognised that they are weakening if continually worn, and interfere with the circulation if too tight. Excluding the surgical, the purposes of the three types in use—stable, working and tail—are discussed below.

Before any bandage is applied, it should be correctly rolled; tapes are attached at one end for fastening, and the bandages should be rolled tightly and evenly from here, with the tapes folded inside. Beginning on the outside of the limb, and pressing the end of the bandage against it with the left hand, pass the roll closely round the leg with the right until the starting point is reached; now the left hand, still holding the end in place, takes the roll while the right is brought back. From here onwards the bandage is unrolled in a downward spiral, the left hand always holding in place the previous turn, which is overlapped by the next by about half its width. When the required distance has been covered, unroll in an upward spiral until the first turn is covered, then tie the tapes around the leg, finishing with a secure bow on the outside, and tucking in the ends. If tied on the inside it may be rubbed undone by the shoe of the opposite foot, and if tied on the tendon, may raise a lump. No turn should be tighter than the previous one, nor should the tapes be tighter than the bandage.

Stable Bandages. These can be used for warmth during illness; as a covering for surgical bandages, to keep them clean and in position; and as a protection from injury when travelling in a road or rail box. Their use in cases of "filled" legs (that is, swollen, usually through inactivity) can scarcely be defended; the correct procedure with any complaint is to treat the cause, not the symptom.

The bandages should be removed twice daily and the legs hand-rubbed to guard against interference with the circulation.

They are of wool, flannel, or a mixture of wool and cotton, in grey or some other dark colour, about seven or eight feet long by three or four inches wide. Since they must not affect the circulation, they should not be put on any tighter than is necessary to keep them in place, and a layer of cotton wool beneath is recommended, as a precaution against pressure and as additional warmth or protection. They should extend from immediately below the knee or hock, over the fetlock and pastern, to the coronet. It will be found impossible to make them lie smoothly over the pastern joint, but any loose folds here will be covered by the following turn.

Working Bandages. These can be used as protection for the legs and tendons during work where injury is likely—as in fast work and jumping—but are unnecessary for normal exercise. Good, sound tendons need no support in ordinary work. They should be left on no longer than they are needed.

Working bandages are of stockinette, or other elastic material, usually white, and about five or six feet long by 3½ or 4 inches wide. Being elastic, and applied over cotton wool, they can be tighter than stable bandages, and should extend from just under the knee or hock to the fetlock joint without interfering with the movement of either. The tapes must be tight enough to prevent their working loose. Sufficient of the surplus cotton wool showing above and below the bandage should be pulled out to make the final effect neat, leaving about half-an-inch visible.

Tail Bandages. It seems that a groom's or horsekeeper's education is incomplete unless he has mastered the art of enclosing the top of the tail in a tight bandage. There may, however, be infrequent occasions when a tail bandage is excusable, purely as a guard against damage, such as with a horse that continually rubs its tail, or when travelling in a box.

Most horsemen use any handy material, but wool is usual. The bandage should cover about three-quarters of the length of the dock, must not be tighter than necessary, and must not be worn continually. The last two turns are carried over the first, around the root of the tail, the tapes finishing in a bow on top, with the ends tucked in. To remove, slide the whole off down the tail.

KNEE AND HOCK CAPS

These are generally only used for protection when travelling, although knee caps are sometimes also fitted for exercise with a horse that is expected to stumble. They are made of strong wool or felt with leather bosses over the knee joint or the point of the hock, or of leather throughout lined with wool or other soft material, and shaped to fit the joints and not interfere with their movement. Two straps are provided; the upper one, padded on the inside, fitting above the joint tightly enough to keep the cap in position, the lower one, unpadded, encircling the leg loosely below the joint. Care must be taken in fitting Knee Caps that they keep in place but allow free trotting movement.

10

Tricks and vices

It is definitely a fact that horses are seldom vicious by nature, but many become so, due to bad treatment in one form or another. In some cases the trouble may be traced back to rough and unsympathetic handling by the breaker, in others to bad stable management, teasing, evidence of fear by those in charge, or, only too often, to downright ill-treatment.

What may be termed "bad habits" are frequently acquired, either during the early stages of training, in which case they prove difficult to cure, or later in imitation of other horses. Certain tricks or bad habits are in other cases obviously inherited, whilst some are due to temperament.

To cure these tricks and vices many methods, both simple and complicated, have been devised and a few of the more simple ones will be mentioned here, but it has been proved that the best results are obtained in all cases by good stable management and, above all, by sensible, sympathetic yet firm handling. Find, if you can, the cause of the trouble and then proceed, by commonsense means, to put things right and it is probable you will have no need to resort to the more drastic methods.

Biting. This, fortunately, is not a very common vice, although many horses will make playful snatches and nips on certain occasions. This is little to worry about, but may develop unpleasantly and should not be aggravated by teasing. Make allowances for ticklish spots and be gentle there, but at the same time firmly check any tendency towards nipping.

Many stallions are natural biters, and care should be taken walking past their box. It is for this reason that bars are sometimes placed across the top half of the stable door.

If you have a vicious biter to contend with, the sort that lays back his ears, shows the whites of his eyes and really tries to get you, it is probable that mere firm treatment will have little effect. There are several ways of dealing with an animal of this kind. For grooming, tying him up short so that he cannot reach you will be sufficient. Other ways are the use of the muzzle or the "side-stick". The side-stick is a stick of suitable thickness and length attached to the noseband of the headcollar and to the pad of a surcingle, to restrict movement. Both muzzle and side-stick must, of course, be removed for feeding, etc. or when not actually required.

There is one other means which not only checks biting but may also help to cure it. This is a snaffle bit of thick wood or hard rubber, which causes the horse a certain amount of pain when he bites on it.

Crib Biting and Windsucking. These two vices may, with advantage, be considered together and, in fact, they not infrequently accompany each other.

The crib-biter grips with the teeth any available fitting, such as a manger, at the same time gulping down air, whilst the wind-sucker swallows air without gripping a fixed object. Thus it will be seen at once that attempting to cure crib-biting merely by removing all fittings may lead to windsucking. No permanent cure of either can be guaranteed, but a recent development in veterinary surgery gives satisfactory results with young horses.

These two vices often cause indigestion and colic, and crib-biting results in rapid and excessive wearing down of the teeth with resultant loss of condition.

The primary cause will usually prove to be idleness and boredom or it may be imitation of another horse. The first three steps, then, are obvious:

(1) Give regular work or keep the horse out of the stable in some way as much as possible. When he must stand in for any length of time let him have a net of hay to pick at and keep him occupied. Do not make the mistake of providing a salt lick under the impression this will serve the same purpose; it may in some instances, but on the other hand it has been known to encourage the trouble or even to cause it in the first place.

(2) Allow him no opportunity of passing the habit on to others.

(3) Remove all fittings so that there is nothing for him to grasp. Anything that cannot be removed should be

smeared with unpleasant tasting stuff such as soap or aloes and treacle. Muzzling may be necessary except at feeding times.

These should be sufficient for our crib biter, if he is curable, but more may be required to prevent windsucking. The object here must be to prevent the swallowing of air, and to stop him arching his neck for this purpose. This is often done with a gullet plate and cribbing strap, which a saddler can supply. Better still, perhaps, is the "flute bit" which is also obtainable from a saddler; this has a perforated hollow mouthpiece and effectively prevents air being sucked in.

Crib-biting or windsucking may sometimes be developed from a habit of licking the walls, which, again, is quite often due to boredom, and regular work is then the remedy. In other instances, however, the fault lies in the food, which may be inadequate, or with insufficient bulk or lack of minerals. It may, perhaps, be traced to internal parasites and when these are cleared from the system the habit will disappear.

Kicking. The problem of the kicker is one that receives, possibly, too little attention; that such-and-such a horse is a kicker is so often accepted as an unpleasant but unalterable fact, no steps being taken to find out the reason and deal with it accordingly. What is generally the reaction to such a horse? Nine times out of ten it is, "Look out for that one, he kicks!" or "Give him a taste of the 'old one-two'"—reaching for a whip. This attitude does not get one very far. First, endeavour to find the cause; there is a reason for everything and therefore, barring exceptional and some long-standing cases, there is a cure.

It is an accepted fact that mares are more likely to kick than geldings, but this usually shows itself during the œstrus period when, obviously, allowances must be made and due care taken not to aggravate ticklishness. With considerate handling the tendency to kick at these times will gradually decrease and eventually disappear completely. Bullying is no help in such circumstances.

Another cause of kicking in the stable can be lack of work and boredom.

In the heavier horses, particularly, "itchy heels" are often the root of the trouble. With proper care and attention this will not arise.

It is not unreasonable that kicking may be expected from a youngster with a strenuous objection to being handled, and such an animal must be taught he has nothing to fear. The "old one-two" could hardly be described as a remedy for him, he needs to be handled regularly and to be accustomed to having what he probably regards as "liberties" taken with him. Should he be very difficult, try stroking his hindquarters with the padded end of a long pole. Carried out daily, this will soon convince him there is no cause for fear.

Vermin scuttling about the stable may be the culprits when there is kicking at night-time, hence the stable cat's uses.

A few horses do not like the dark and show their disapproval in the usual way. Introducing a dim light of a safe kind, placed well out of harm's way, will immediately put the matter right. For safety and convenience it is worth while investing in a low-powered electric lamp run from a car battery with reliable leads and connections.

Strange horses in the next box will occasionally cause kicking at first but this can be expected to right itself as soon as they are no longer strangers. Lose no time in bringing this about as kicking can soon develop into a vice.

Kicking while being groomed is in most cases traced to ticklishness, particularly with thin-skinned animals. The only possible course is extra care when dealing with the more sensitive parts. If the trouble is really serious, and nothing else has any effect, one foreleg can be either held up by another person or strapped up. Since the horse can only stand on three legs for a short time, he should be given opportunities of resting now and then. As an added precaution, provide a thick bed during these operations in case the horse should lose balance.

Lastly, mischievousness may be the beginning of kicking which ends as a vice, and a sharp but fair reminder of stable manners is not out of place. When such a lesson is called for, it need be no more than a sharp rap on the leg that is raised to strike but it should be administered as soon as the leg is moved for kicking. Prompt action of this kind has been known to cure horses for all time of kicking during grooming, at one lesson. The value of the use of the voice should not be overlooked, the tone being suited to the nature of the case.

Whatever the cause, if kicking at partitions or posts shows signs of continuing, it is an excellent idea to pad these parts with coarse matting, which will not only prevent injury but also deaden the noise; many horses derive great satisfaction from the sound of their own kicking and are encouraged to greater efforts. It will be noticed that in some stables bunches of gorse or other prickly stuff are used instead of padding so that the horse shall associate pain with kicking and therefore desist. This may effect a cure, or the pain may quite probably cause worse kicking, so if you decide to try this method, watch results carefully.

In connection with kicking at persons, it is worth noting that swishing of the tail is a warning sign, when there are no flies about, and that the nearer one is to the animal when he strikes out, the less is the force of the blow. In grooming the hindlegs it is always wise to make a habit of grasping the hamstring with the free hand, when tension of the leg for a lash-out can be felt in time and the kick prevented by putting the weight on the hamstring and hock.

Rough treatment of a kicker never produces good results, it will be remembered and repaid with interest at the first opportunity.

Weaving. A horse is said to be a weaver when he constantly swings his head, neck and forehand from side to side, almost invariably over the bottom half of the door. In some cases only the head and neck are swung to and fro, producing an effect that reminds one of a spectator at a tennis match, whilst in others the horse actually rocks, often lifting one forefoot after the other or even crossing them.

There is little doubt that weaving is a nervous habit and it is one which is most frequently noticed in wild animals kept in captivity, from which it may be deduced that dislike of being shut in, coupled with boredom and idleness, is the root of the matter.

From a horse keeper's point of view, the main objection to the habit is that the constant motion of the head and neck is wasted energy. In addition, it is regarded as an unsoundness and there is evidence to show that it is hereditary.

Once formed, the habit of weaving is not easy to break and the owner of several horses may have to guard against imitation by the other occupants of the stable. Attempts are usually made to check the trouble by preventing lateral movement of the head by means of short pillar reins, but this is merely treating the symptom instead of the cause. The first thing to do is to ensure that the animal has sufficient regular work or exercise and that he does not spend unnecessarily long periods idle in the stable. To this end, as much use as possible must be made of any available grazing in suitable weather; it will frequently be found that such a horse is a "bad-doer" in the stable but picks up wonderfully and is far more "alive" at his work when kept in the open. At such times as he has to be stabled, let there be something to occupy his attention, a hay-net or even a salt lick—in the case of a weaver a salt lick seldom leads to the other vices of crib-biting or gnawing at walls. Imitation of weaving by others is not such a danger as many think and it is debatable whether it is wise to keep a weaver away from his companions, as in doing so one is liable to aggravate the trouble. However, watch other animals carefully and at the first sign of their picking up the habit, remove the first offender.

It would be unwise to guarantee a permanent cure, it having been found that weavers which have spent years at grass immediately resume the old habit when they are back in the stable—possibly for the reason given before. However, many good horses are confirmed weavers and show no sign of the loss of condition usually foretold for their kind.

11
The composition of foods and suitable rations

IN his natural state, the horse satisfied all his food requirements from grass, but he was able to change his pasture at will to find the best food, and seldom travelled at more than a walking pace, grazing as he went, except in escaping from enemies. Under domestication his size has increased and he is required to work, therefore needing a more concentrated diet, in a balanced form, to maintain a larger body and supply additional energy.

To understand the requirements of a balanced ration it is necessary first to know something about the constituents of food, which, for animal feeding, may be grouped into five recognised classifications. It is not enough, however, to supply concentrated nourishment alone; owing to the nature of his digestive apparatus, bulk is essential. The constituents and their uses are:—

Proteins. These are flesh-formers, nitrogenous compounds which are split up and simplified by the processes of digestion into a form which the bloodstream is capable of absorbing. Their purpose is mainly to make good the normal wear of tissues and provide for growth. A deficiency will be met by the system robbing the muscles of protein, while too much will lead to ill effects on the digestion and skin, diarrhœa from irritation in the intestines, and strain on the kidneys. A slight excess, however, can be stored by the body as a reserve of energy. Examples in horse feeding are beans and peas, which are rich in protein to the extent of about 25 per cent of their composition, and valuable when great exertion is required, as in racehorses and hunters, but if supplied in large quantities are "heating" and cause disorders of the digestive system.

Fats and Carbohydrates. For nutritive purposes these are comparable with each other and have similar functions, producing heat to maintain the body temperature, energy for work, and adding to the reserve store of fat and energy. They are present in all green foods and grain; linseed is particularly rich in fats, with a percentage of 35 to 40 in the whole seeds, and about 10 in the cake. Carbohydrates exist in oats (which are also rich in digestible oil), barley and maize at 57 to 70 per cent, while beans and peas contain about 50 per cent.

Minerals. These bone-forming salts are essential for youngsters, hence the popularity of limestone soils where grass has a large content, and they are also necessary for other stock. Common salt is a form in which they may be easily added to the food, at the rate of about an ounce per day, either mixed with the food or dissolved in water and sprinkled over the hay. With best quality foods it should not be necessary to add salt as these will contain sufficient. In addition to grass and hay from suitable soils, minerals are contained in most leguminous plants and in bone meal, whilst cereals are deficient in them, maize and wheat 1.5 per cent, oats 3 per cent.

Fibre. Although supplying some energy and fat, the chief use of fibre is to provide bulk and assist in the digestion of concentrated foods. Its value in horse feeding also lies in the distension of the stomach and capacious intestines, giving that necessary "comfortable" feeling. Hay and straw supply the greatest bulk, being 25 to 35 per cent fibre but straw has practically negligible food value. (See page 70.)

Water. Water is the commonest but most important of all foods; animals can live longer without solid food than without water. Its functions are to aid digestion and cleanse the system. The greatest percentage is found in roots and grass (75 to 90 per cent), but an unstinted supply is always necessary, since horses drink from eight to fifteen gallons daily. Horses are normally "fussy" about water; it must be clean and free from any odour or taint, and soft is preferred to hard, although the latter is often recommended for growing stock on account of the lime content.

In addition to the foregoing, the ration must contain small percentages of the various vitamins. These are obtained naturally when grazing, hence the enormous value of "green meat" fed to stabled horses. Brief details are given in the following table:

Vitamin.	*Purpose.*	*Source.*
"A"	Growth and protection from infection.	Green Foods and Carrots.
"B"	Growth, nervous system and heart.	Green Foods, Roots and Grain.
"C"	Healthy Blood Supply.	Green Foods.
"D"	Healthy Bones and Teeth.	Notably Cod Liver Oil —a valuable addition to the diet of growing stock.

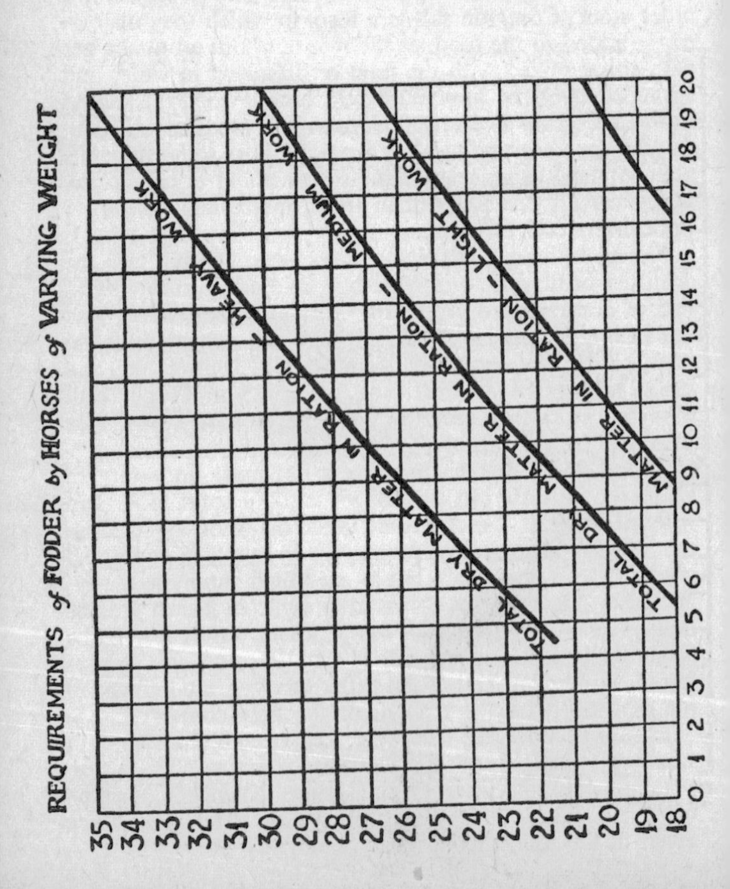

Balanced Rations

A balanced ration is one containing certain proportions of proteins, fats, carbohydrates and fibre, together with a percentage of minerals and vitamins. The suitability of a ration for the type of horse and his work is often esti-

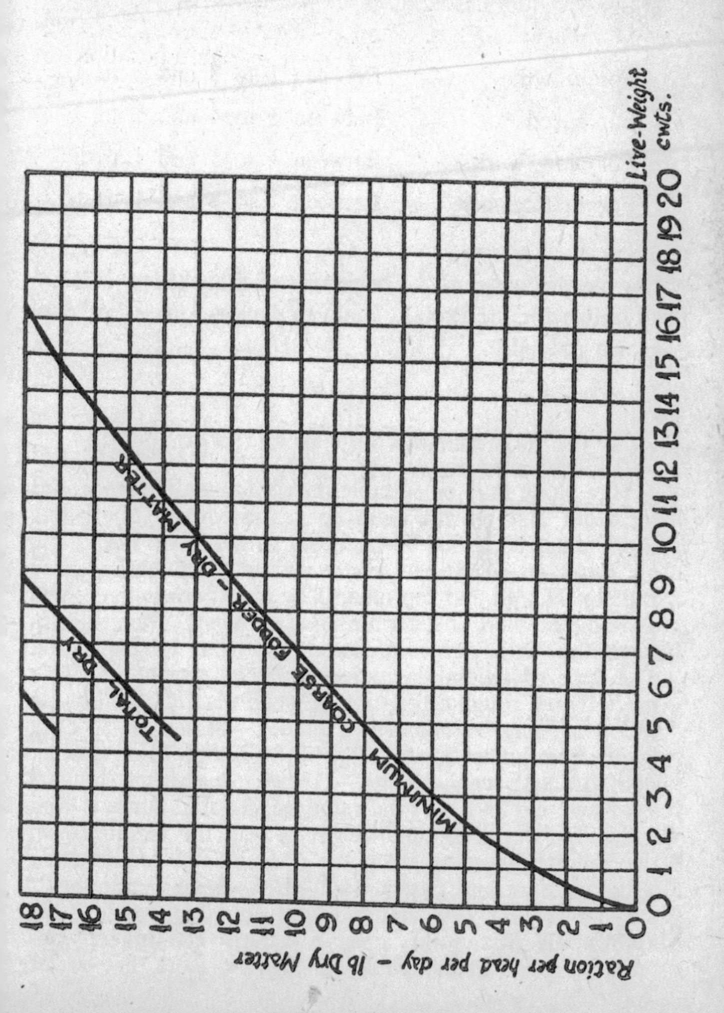

mated by its Protein or Nitrogenous Ratio, that is, the proportion of true, digestible protein to fats, carbohydrates and fibre (see Table on page 70).

The following are the ratios generally considered suitable:

For growth.	Between 1 to 3 and 1 to 4.
For speed.	Between 1 to 4 and 1 to 5.
For slow work.	Between 1 to 5 and 1 to 8.
For maintenance.	Between 1 to 8 and 1 to 10.

For reasons given at the beginning of this chapter it is not advisable for the Protein Ratio to exceed 1 to 4 for fully-grown animals.

Maintenance and Work Rations

Hay alone may be suitable purely for maintenance, but for work and growth more concentrated and nourishing foods must be added—oats being found best. The graph on pages 66/67, issued in the Ministry of Agriculture's Bulletin No. 48 and reproduced by kind permission, offers a simple method of determining approximate quantities of foods for various types of horses according to their work. The type of animal is indicated by its weight in cwts.; more than a rough estimation of weight is difficult, but the following may be taken as a guide:—Shires 18–20 cwt., heavy farm horses 15 cwt., light farm horses 13 cwt., other light draught, vanners, etc., 11 cwt., hacks and hunters 9–11 cwt. To find the food required, the first curve is consulted for the minimum weight of hay for maintenance; the following curves show the concentrates required for light, medium and heavy work. These food requirements are shown as "dry matter", and for true weights the appropriate percentages must be added. Dry matter contents are given in the Table on page 70. Note that horses over 16 years normally need a slightly higher proportion of concentrates.

Examples:

Ration for a hunter of about 11 cwt:

Maintenance. The first curve shows 14 lbs. Hay contains 85 per cent dry matter, therefore about 2 lbs. must be added $(\frac{15}{100} \times 14)$	16 lbs. Hay.
Light Work. The first curve, as above, shows	16 lbs. Hay.
The second curve shows 20 lbs., of which hay accounted for 14 lbs., leaving 6 lbs. concentrates. Oats contain 86.7 per cent dry matter, therefore about 1 lb. must be added	7 lbs. Oats.
	23 lbs. Total.

Oat Equivalents

Oats being accepted as the standard concentrate, it is convenient to be able to compare other foods with them. For instance, if we wish to replace a proportion of the oat ration with, say, malt culms, we must know this food's oat value or "oat equivalent". This has been assessed from the Starch Equivalent, that is, the energy value of 100 lbs. of a given food compared with starch, and listed in the Table on next page. From this we see that the Oat Equivalent of Malt Culms is 13.5, which means that 13.5 lbs. of Malt Culms are equal to 10 lbs. of oats. By applying this information to the graph, the horse keeper will be able to work out in a few minutes feeding programmes to suit foods available and work required.

FOODS—COMPOSITION, PROTEIN RATIO, STARCH AND OAT EQUIVALENTS.

	*Dry Matter.** *(Per cent)*	*Starch Equiv.** *(Per cent)*	*Protein** *Ratio*	*Oat Equiv.* *Per* 10 *lbs*
Oats.	86.7	59.5	1 to 7	10
Bran.	87.0	42.6	1 to 4	14
Hay—Meadow.	85.0	32.0	1 to 11	—
Hay—Seeds.	86.0	30.0	1 to 6	—
Straw—Oat.	86.0	20–21	1 to 16–67	—
Beans.	85.7	65.8	1 to 2	9
Soya Beans.	90.0	78.9	1 to 2	7.5
Peas.	86.0	69.0	1 to 3	8.6
Maize.	87.0	77.6	1 to 9	7.7
Maize—Flaked.	89.0	84.0	1 to 8	7.0
Linseed—Seeds.	92.9	119.2	1 to 5	5.0
Linseed—Cake.	88.8	74.0	1 to 2	8.0
Cotton Cake Dec.	90.2	68.4	1 to 1	8.7
Barley.	85.1	71.4	1 to 9	8.3
Wheat.	86.6	71.6	1 to 7	8.3
Rye.	86.6	71.6	1 to 7	8.3
Malt Culms.	90.0	43.4	1 to 3	13.5
Brewers' Gns.—Wet.	32.4	18.4	1 to 3	32.0
Brewers' Gns.—Dried.	89.7	48.3	1 to 4	12.3
Fresh Grass.	20–33	13.4–14	1 to 4.8–11	—
Carrots.	13.0	8.8	1 to 12	—
Swedes.	11.5	7.3	1 to 7	—
Mangolds.	10.7–13.2	5.5–6.8	1 to 11–14	—
Turnips.	8.5	4.4	1 to 9	—
Dried Grass.	90.0	60.3–65.7	1 to 3.3–4.8	9.98

* The figures in the first three columns are extracted from the Ministry of Agriculture Bulletin No. 48 by kind permission.

12

Types of foods and their uses

THE first three of the following, oats, bran and hay (including chaff), are the main items of horse-feed in normal circumstances, whilst others are special-purpose ingredients to be sparingly used. Certain grains, also mentioned, have been occasionally substituted satisfactorily for oats.

Oats. The best oats are the white variety, and they should have the minimum of husk and be plump, short, hard and dry. Oats are preferred at least a year old, since they need to mature and dry out, and the slight chemical changes taking place in new oats give rise to fermentation.

It has been found from experience that oats are the best grain for horses, being easily digested and having great energy value. Of all corn it is the most liked, and, apart from its known feeding qualities, has tonic effects which are not yet completely understood. In some instances these effects produce such stimulation, amounting almost to inebriation, that the animals can be allowed very little, and although these cases are comparatively rare, discretion must always be used and the supply carefully regulated according to exercise and work. The graph on pages 66/67 shows suitable amounts. If the correct ration is exceeded beyond the amount which the body can store in the form of a heat and energy reserve, digestive troubles may follow. In cases of enforced idleness, through weather conditions or other such circumstances, the ration must be decreased in proportion to the time spent in the stable, and during illness or injury it must be completely excluded from the diet until authorised by the Veterinary Surgeon. During this time, damped bran and an extra amount of hay should comprise the feed. When eventually permitted, the allowance of oats should be added gradually in small quantities to avoid digestive upsets.

It is unusual but oats can be fed whole except to

youngsters, old horses or those with teeth or digestive troubles. However, it will be noticed that, when fed whole, a certain proportion of oats always pass through the body without undergoing action by the digestive system and can be detected in the droppings. Therefore, being an expensive item and one from which all possible nutrition should be extracted, it is always advisable to feed oats crushed—not flattened, but sufficiently split so that the flour inside can be acted upon by the gastric juices—otherwise the husk, not easily masticated, prevents complete digestion and a proportion will pass through whole. If crushed oats are unobtainable, or facilities for crushing are not available, they may be steamed or boiled to soften or split the husk, and fed when cool, in which way they are much relished. It must be pointed out, however, that boiling any food may destroy valuable vitamins, and the constant use of boiled foods leads to over-distension of the stomach; steaming is safer, that is, soaking with hot water. These remarks do not, of course, apply to linseed.

Bulk must be added in the form of chaff (chopped hay or oat straw), together with bran (broad is best), not only to compel mastication but also to satisfy the digestive system's need for distension. As a guide only, the proportions may be put at one half of oats to one quarter each of bran and chaff, or one half oats to one half chaff, plus long hay.

At one time, due to transport and other difficulties attendant upon war and its aftermath, it was not possible to obtain sufficient of the normal foods. Oats were strictly rationed, and certain types of so-called "non-working" horses were allowed none. As a result the less fortunate, and the more law-abiding, horse keepers were compelled to look around for improvisations. As a matter of interest, and possible value, some of these alternatives are given in Chapter 13, "Substitute Feeding".

Oatmeal Gruel. As a "pick-me-up" after exhausting work, or on the way home from hunting, gruel can be made from oatmeal by scalding two or three handfuls, allowing to cool before feeding. Or it may be made quickly by simply mixing thoroughly in a bucket of cold water to make a thin paste.

Bran. This is the offal of wheat milling, and for horse feeding *broad* bran is preferred. A glance at the table on page 70 will show that for animals its feeding value is high (the human digestive system is unable to extract from it a similar degree of nourishment). Bran is not noted for "keeping" qualities, and quickly absorbs moisture from the atmosphere; it should therefore be bought only in reasonable quantities—especially in view of the fact that normally the cost is a little more than that of oats. Bran is perhaps usually thought of as a pick-me-up for tired or "off-colour" animals when fed as a mash. In this form it is also a mild laxative and used to be a regular Saturday evening meal (fed dry it has the opposite effect). A bran mash is made by scalding half a bucketful of bran with sufficient boiling water to be absorbed, stirring well; the bucket is then covered with a sack or blanket so that the bran cools slowly and "cooks". When cool enough to eat, it is fed without further addition, but to make it more palatable a small handful of salt can be stirred in. If the mash is refused at first, mix a handful of oats in at the top, but otherwise no hard food should be included as it "slides down" without chewing.

Hay. The growing practice of ensiling grass (see Silage, Chapter 13) leads to occasional shortage of hay, and horse keepers are strongly advised to take every opportunity of making their own.

It is one of the most useful forms of forage, and the only one on which alone a horse can live and perform some slow, light work. Straw does not supply sufficient energy even to replace that expended in its mastication and digestion, and is therefore not a substitute. The quality of hay varies considerably; well made and kept it has a valuable feeding content, but otherwise can be useless or even injurious. Of the types, clover, meadow and seed (or "mixture", that is, from a ley), choice is a matter of individual preference, there being little difference in nutritional value, but they offer an easy way of introducing variety.

Old hay is safer to use than new, since the latter is still "making" or undergoing chemical change, and may upset the stomach. However, ill effects are rare and as long as the possibility is realised and the first indication of them watched for, new hay may be safely fed if circumstances dictate. In the trade, hay is regarded as old after Michaelmas Day (29th September)—it is well to know this when dealing with forage merchants—but, broadly, the previous year's crop may be considered as old, that is, from six to eighteen months after cutting. After that time much of its usefulness is lost.

To recognise good hay, note its appearance, smell ("nose"), taste and feel. It is never yellow; meadow hay, cut at the right time and well saved, is greenish when new, but fading slowly with age, and with the colour of any flowers retained. Seed hay is lighter in colour, and clover darker. Dark brown or black patches indicate dampness or "burning". Meadow hay, and sometimes seed, has a distinctive "nose", familiar to all, particularly strong when much sweet vernal is present, but the aroma decreases with age. The taste should be slightly sweet, never bitter. In feel, meadow hay is soft, seed and clover harsher and more brittle. There should be the minimum of thistles, nettles, docks, sorrel and other weeds. Ragwort (*Senecio jacobaea*) is a common pasture weed and causes very severe effects on horses if it is consumed in the hay. Note if the sample is dusty; clover especially often becomes dusty with age or if badly made.

These days, dusty hay is becoming common and merchants are reluctant to replace or credit it; when circumstances compel its use, such hay should be sprinkled with water before feeding.

The forage can be bought in trusses (trade weight 56 lbs. new and 60 lbs. old hay) or in bales (approximately 80 lbs.). The latter, being more compressed, are easier to store but unless the sample is good and was baled dry do not keep so well; rusty baling wire should lead to a careful examination of the hay before acceptance. When buying in the stack, the approximate weight can be quickly guessed by taking 10 cubic yards as one ton.

Feeding Hay: It is commonly said that to feed long hay is wasteful, much being lost by trampling or by the wind when in the open, and it is therefore frequently the practice to chaff most if not all of it. Undoubtedly the horse gets more satisfaction from long hay, and one cannot feed chaff alone—particularly at night. The use of nets avoids practically all loss, besides compelling slower eating, and is strongly advised. (See also page 23.) First shake the hay up well, or tease it out, to make feeding easier, to get rid of dust and to detect foreign bodies (dangerous articles such as sticks, lengths of briar, pieces of barbed wire, etc., often find their way in). If this is done over a small tarpaulin, or something similar, the seeds that fall can be added to the chaff supply and, especially with mixture hay, a great saving will be effected. By pushing it well down, 10 to 12 lbs. of hay can easily be put into each net. When hanging up for feeding, tie at a height where there will be no danger of a horse catching a foot in the net, but not so high that he must imitate a giraffe and have his eyes filled with seeds and small bits. Very few people, even

TYING A HAY NET

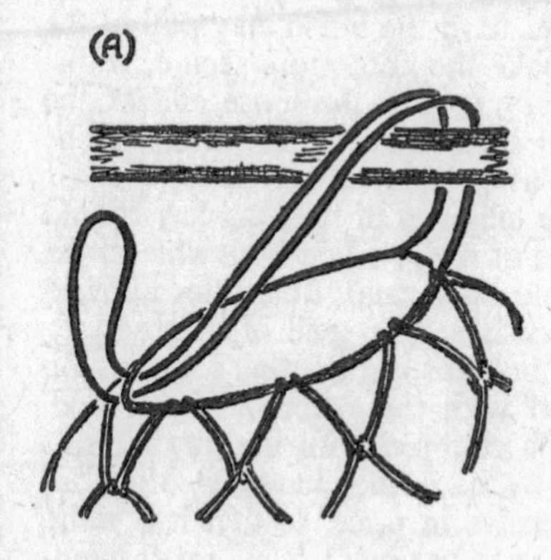

(A)
Drawstring passed around bar and through net.

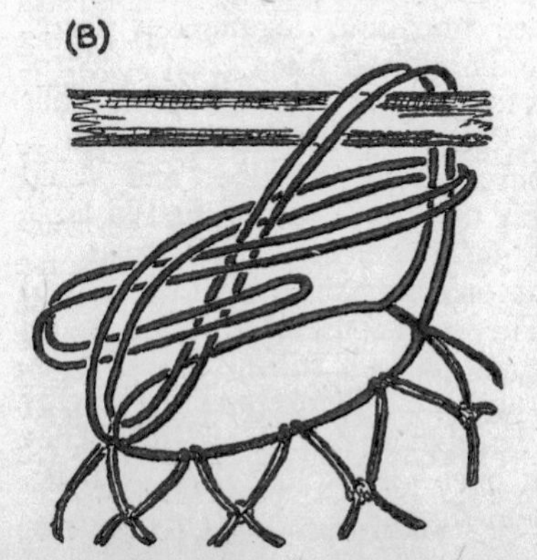

(B)
Drawstring encircles itself and is looped through. Drawstring should be tightened and net pulled close up to bar. Pull loop to tighten; end can be passed through loop for security.

To Untie: Pull free end after removing from loop.

otherwise experienced, seem able to tie a net well so that it stays tied and at the original height. A quick release knot is used, and the procedure is:—Having filled the net, first pull the draw-string as tight as possible, pushing the hay down; pass this doubled string over the branch or bar selected and pull it to raise the net right up; supporting the net, *thread the draw-string through its opposite end on the net* (figure "A"); pass it round the two double lengths now formed between the bar and the net until it meets itself, then make a loop and pass through between that part brought from the bar back to the net and the part returning to encircle the two double lengths—only far enough to take a finger (figure "B"); now pull the loop to tighten the whole. However hard the horse may pull at the net, the only effect is to make the knot more secure, whilst to untie it is only necessary to jerk the loose end of the drawstring. For additional security, the loose end may be passed through the loop as a "keeper".

For a working horse the majority of the long hay should be given after the last feed at night, when he is able to eat and digest it at leisure, and only small quantities allowed during the day unless there is a long spell of inactivity.

About a quarter (say 3 or 4 lbs.) of the day's hay ration can be chaffed and mixed with the grain or other food, and frequently oat straw is chopped with the hay for this purpose. Chaff supplied by corn merchants is often inferior in quality and expensive in price, so that it is more economical and satisfactory to cut one's own; small hand-power machines are cheap to buy and soon save their cost.

Beans and Peas. These nutritious leguminous seeds, rich in the proteins, are only advised when great speed or hard work have to be performed, or when an animal falls away badly in condition. They are also useful in cases where there is long exposure to severe weather, and would be valuable to horses living out in the winter. Fed in large quantities they are "heating", and the ration must not exceed 2 or 3 lbs. daily, according to the size of the animal and the circumstances. They make useful addition to fill the nitrogen deficiency when maize is substituted for oats.

The varieties are Soya and Field Beans, and white, grey or blue peas; all should be light in colour and dry. They should be a year old and have their tough skins split before feeding, to make them digestible.

Bean Meal can also be used, and gruel made from it for the same purpose and in the same way as oatmeal gruel.

Maize. This is a carbohydrate grain, and is mostly used for horses at heavy work, when it may take the place of oats but must have the addition of nitrogenous grains. It can be estimated that ¾ lb. of maize contains as much nutriment as 1 lb. of oats, and a mixture consisting of two-thirds maize and one-third beans has roughly one-and-a-quarter times the feeding value of oats. Maize is unsuitable for horses at fast work or those with little work, and tends to form fat. Being indigestible, it should always be kibbled or crushed, and the flaked form is popular in stables; whole maize may be fed, but it is better softened by soaking or boiling in this case. Owing to the time required for digestion, it is not advisable to allow water within at least two hours of feeding.

As a general rule, maize is fed in the same proportions as oats, but it is better to limit the ration to an average of about 2 lbs. daily, balancing with other foods such as oats, beans or peas, and including a more generous allowance of chaff to compel mastication.

Linseed. A nutritious food, the seed of the flax plant, is useful for putting on fat and improving the appearance of the coat—many stables feeding it while the coat is being changed—but is particularly valuable, boiled, to tempt the appetite during illness or when there is inflammation of any part of the digestive tract. Having a marked effect on poor condition, boiled linseed is also used with advantage when recovering from illness, and is excellent mixed with boiled barley. It is obtainable in four forms, cake, whole seeds, meal and oil.

Cake is made from seed from which the greatest possible amount of oil has been expressed, and is merely the residue of the process. It may be crushed and fed dry, when ½ to 1 lb. makes a useful addition to the daily ration of a bad-doer, or it may be scalded to make linseed tea for moistening the other food.

Seeds and meal, in the same amount, are greedily eaten as mashes, but care must be taken in their preparation. *On no account should they be given unboiled,* as prussic acid is present in the moist, warm state. It is better to mix these mashes with bran mash, since, being slimy, they may be swallowed without chewing. The whole seeds can be boiled, with constant stirring to prevent burning, until they burst and form a sticky jelly. This takes several hours and a more convenient way is to soak them in cold water for 24 hours, subsequently boiling for about ten minutes. Linseed meal may be soaked in cold water for about a quarter of that time and boiled for two hours. In all cases the remaining water should be fed as linseed tea.

The oil form is not easily digested and for most horses is an acquired taste, but has beneficial effects on condition if mixed with the food at the rate of one to two tablespoonsful daily. It is also a mild laxative and may be given in minor cases of colic.

Cotton Cake. Although better known as a cattle food, the decorticated form (from which the husks of the seeds have been removed) is sometimes used for horses. It has a high protein content and is fed in the same way as linseed cake. The undecorticated cake is unsuitable, being liable to become mouldy and cause digestive trouble.

"Feeding Nuts." There are various brands of nuts or "cubes" on the market, most of which are excellent foods with a high protein and mineral content and with essential vitamins added. Besides having great nutritional value without the "alcoholic" effects of oats, they are suitable for and liked by all classes of horses, including breeding and growing stock. Feeding nuts offer a very convenient form of balanced and concentrated food, although unfortunately they are perhaps slightly expensive, and can be highly recommended in place of all or part of the oat ration, together with the usual amount of hay and chaff. It is fed dry in the same quantities as oats or may be made into a mash with bran.

Other Grain for Horses

Barley. This grain is not very much used for horse-feeding in Great Britain, except boiled for "poor" animals, but has been found quite satisfactory in many other countries, or where oats have not been available. In the Middle East, British cavalry horses were able to thrive and perform their exhausting duties on a sole grain diet of whole barley, contrary to all our preconceived ideas.

Whenever possible, however, barley should be crushed or soaked for a day and boiled until soft, to make it more digestible, and should be fed in rather smaller quantities than oats. Barley meal may also be utilised when obtainable, or the by-products of malting mentioned under "Substitute Feeding".

Barley water, prepared from the meal or from pearl barley, is useful as a soothing drink for inflammation of the throat or gullet, or when there is a high temperature. Two or three ounces should be simmered in a quart of water for a couple of hours, strained and then allowed to cool.

Wheat. Wheat is rarely fed to horses and is generally said to be unsuitable; price and the demand for human consumption are against it, and oats are better liked. It could quite safely be used in small quantities, provided it was thoroughly dry, crushed and mixed with plenty of bulk. Although condemned as causing laminitis, if fed with care—particularly at first—wheat is unlikely to have ill effects.

Rye. This, very similar in analysis to wheat, is also little used in this country but is not an uncommon horse food in some places abroad. When ground or cooked it can be fed in small quantities like wheat.

13
Substitute feeding

As previously mentioned, one-time shortages of the usual foods led to investigation of suitable substitutes. Some of these substitutes are dealt with in this chapter, and their feeding values are shown in the table on page 70. The consideration of analysis is not "crankiness" but plain commonsense in the circumstances, as are also the inclusion of such things as Bone Meal to make good mineral deficiency, and Cod Liver Oil for vitamins.

The following are examples of emergency feeding stuffs:

Malt Culms. This by-product of brewing consists of the dried rootlets sprouted from barley in the malting chamber. Samples vary greatly in quality, some being dirty and of inferior feeding value, while others, light brown in colour, with a pleasant smell and easily crumbled, make an excellent food. Being low in lime content, it is not the best food for growing stock without an addition to make good this deficiency—but the same might be said about many other forms of forage. Bone Meal (at the rates specified by the manufacturers) is recommended for this purpose. Horses very quickly become accustomed to malt culms and develop a liking for it. It is best fed scalded, like a bran mash, or at least thoroughly moistened, and mixed with other fodder, at the rate of two double handfuls daily, but should be introduced gradually.

As an ingredient of stable rations it appears to be very little known, or is possibly ignored, but the writer has had considerable experience of it and has found it a satisfactory and inexpensive food, for rearing young stock also, with the addition of an average of 3 ozs. each of Bone and Blood Meals for the latter.

Brewers' Grains. These are also a by-product of brewing, being the refuse of malt. They are obtainable wet or dried, and are liked as a change, or to tempt the appetite, but are unsuitable for hard, fast work. The wet grains should be fed quite fresh as they quickly become sour, and should be mixed with the other forage in the same way as malt culms. Unfortunately dried brewers' grains are not liked by all horses.

Dried Grass Meal. This high protein food is valuable to all horse-owners. Although the price is high, it is economical since it must be used sparingly—up to about one pint measure daily or as the makers advise, mixed with other food. The meal is very fine and needs damping to prevent blowing about, but a "nut" form of similar feeding value can be purchased and this is much easier to feed. Buy only first quality of either.

Silage. Ensilage, or silage making, is the system of keeping cut grass and other green crops fresh for winter feeding, against a shortage of hay or, more particularly, roots. Although silage has the great advantage, in the British climate, that it is not so dependent upon the weather for its making as is hay, some skill is necessary to produce good quality stuff.

For silage on a large scale, special buildings or pits are generally used, but for small quantities of about a ton, any suitable receptacles are sufficient. As close-packing and exclusion of air are essential, circular containers, such as barrels, make the process easier, and it is further simplified if the crops are chaffed. 1 lb. of molasses or treacle is allowed for every cwt. of green food, and is made into a solution of one part in three parts of warm water. Freshly-cut and reasonably clean grass or other succulent foods are tightly packed in the receptacle in layers 6 inches deep, with a sprinkling of the solution between each. The last layer is firmly trodden down, with particular attention to the edges, and a weighted cover placed on top to exclude air. In a few days the process of fermentation causes the mixture to become hot, and the top layer is then spread with 6 inches of earth, tightly packed down, and the cover and weight replaced. To make the container airtight, the cover may be lashed down with straining ropes. When opened for use it may be found there is a small amount of waste in the form of mouldy stuff on top or at the edges, where air has found its way in, and this, of course, must be thrown away.

Silage is fed in winter in the same quantities as hay, but it cannot be expected that poor grass and weeds saved in this way will have any more feeding value than in their original state or than poor hay. The increased popularity of silage is probably due to the difficulties encountered in unfavourable hay-making weather, or to a desire to reduce the acreage under roots for cattle, than any special feeding properties. Palatability is certainly added by the molasses.

Roots. It was previously said that roots are a good medium for the introduction of variety. This is the way most stables think of them, but there is no doubt that a regular allowance, of say 5 lbs. daily, would be of great benefit. Carrots are particularly useful, improving condition and toning up the system. They should be sliced lengthways, since it is said that cut in discs they may cause choking. Other roots, such as mangolds, swedes, turnips, artichokes, etc., though frequently fed whole, are better sliced small, grated or pulped, and mixed with the food, for the same reason.

Potatoes. There are two opinions on the feeding of potatoes: (*a*) that sliced raw they are useful in small quantities (one medium potato, I believe, is recommended); (*b*) that they are dangerous, perhaps poisonous, except when boiled. My own feeling is that, dangerous or not, they are of no interest to horse-masters. Their food value is low, and in such small quantities useless; warning has already been given against boiled foods, and I see no reason for taking chances with ingredients which are in any case of little account, although I understand the Irish make use of boiled potatoes for their horses.

14
System of feeding

THERE is no rule of thumb method in feeding; the most carefully compiled chart can be no more than a rough guide, and one is not expected to follow it slavishly. Circumstances must be taken into account, age, constitution and temperament, work, the time of year, weather conditions, and, not least, unaccountable factors in the make-up of the horse which can only be allowed for from experience with the individual animal. These points, particularly the last, apply equally well to most aspects of horse keeping. It has been truly said that only one man can feed a horse—the one who spends most time with it and understands, more or less, its character and peculiarities. Correct feeding calls for knowledge, experience, observation and intelligent use of observation, but there are certain principles that may be laid down.

Cost of Forage. Buy only the best. Money saved on cheap forage will not balance inferior feeding value, loss of condition and possibly of good health.

Feeding Times. Feeds should be small, frequent and regular; three meals a day is the minimum, four are better, five better still. When possible there should not be more than four hours between meals. The reason for this is that the horse has a small stomach for his size and cannot deal with large quantities, but, his intestines being capacious, bulk is needed. The first feed should be given as early as possible, 6.30 a.m. or 7.30 a.m.; the last, of hay, as late as possible, about 10.30 p.m. (see "Daily Routine", Chapter 5). A horse should not be expected to work for at least an hour after a full feed, and if exceptional circumstances make it impossible to allow this time for digestion, the pace must not be faster than a walk or, owing to the distension of the stomach restricting the free action of the lungs, his wind will suffer, or the stomach may even be ruptured following strenuous work. Nor should a large feed be given immediately on return to stables if the horse is tired, as the digestive system is not then in a condition to function well.

Watering. It is generally accepted that a horse should be watered before feeding, none being allowed for at least an hour after (except in the case of hay, which he will want to moisten with little sips). This rule is good and based on sound reasons: water causes food in the stomach to swell, possibly resulting in colic, and a proportion of the corn will be washed through the system undigested. The objection to this rule is that it is usually too strictly observed and the horse is expected to drink only at set times. He may not be thirsty at the time, or, more commonly, he associates watering with feeding and is too impatient to think about drinking.

There is an alternative, which gives rise to much controversy, that of leaving water always available in the stable. In this case the horse never goes thirsty, but it is often objected that, nine times out of ten, he will take a long drink immediately after feeding.

The solution of a combination of the two methods is so obvious that it is difficult to understand why there should be any arugment. Have water available in the stable but remove the bucket for an hour from feeding time (two hours if maize is fed), and damp the food with a sprinkling of water. This system has put flesh on many "bad-doers".

Water must always be left in the stable over-night; that is the time when he has the bulk of his hay and most needs it—he will probably account for three or four gallons during the night. If expense is not objected to, the automatic drinking bowls advertised offer an excellent method of watering. There are two kinds: one in which the bowls are kept permanently filled by means of a tank and floating ball valve, and the other in which the horse draws his own supply whenever he wants it, by pressing his nose on a small lever in the bowl, which he quickly learns to do. The supply can, of course, be cut off when desired.

With a horse living out, there is a special difficulty. A tank or trough will be used for water; how, then, can one prevent him from drinking his fill immediately after food? This problem will probably only arise once a day, when the corn (or substitute) feed is given, and I have found the answer is to damp the food and leave a small pile of hay with it.

Just as exercise should not immediately follow a feed, so it should also not follow a full drink, for the same reason —unless the work is slow and light. Contrary to general belief, no harm results, as a rule, from a hot and tired horse drinking cold water, but for safety it is better to allow only a few swallows until he has cooled. However, it is the custom in many stables to take the chill off the water in such cases, and to allow for the animal which may prove the exception to the rule, this is recommended. On the other hand, it may be found that some horses dislike artificially warmed water, so once again knowledge of the individual must be the guide.

One thing is certain: a plentiful and pure supply is essential; nothing leads to loss of condition more quickly than insufficient water—remember a working horse will drink up to fifteen gallons a day. "Bad-doers" are often found to be poor drinkers and improve rapidly if they are encouraged to drink more; adding one or two ounces of salt to their food will help.

When watering at a trough, allow the horse sufficient time to drink his fill—with the exceptions already mentioned—do *not* lead him away as soon as he raises his head, he will do so several times before his thirst is quenched. When more than one horse is being watered, follow the old Army rule and do not disturb a slow drinker by allowing other horses to be led away before he has finished.

Changes in Feeding. Occasional variety is beneficial and appreciated, such as the addition of a pound or two of carrots or other roots, or new grass. Grass must be freshly cut, since it begins to heat and ferment almost immediately. Lawn mowings should not be fed, as they cause severe colic. Take every opportunity of giving the stabled horse fresh grass; it has a tonic effect. For an idle horse it may take the place of hay in quantities up to 50 lbs.

Make any change gradually to allow the system time to adjust itself, especially when changing from grazing to hard food, or vice versa, or digestive disorders will follow. A horse brought in from grass should be fed at first on a little damped bran, say 2 lbs., three or four times a day, with nightly hay, until the droppings indicate by their colour and consistency that the stomach is accustoming itself to the change. (See "Signs of Health", page 135.) Then gradually reduce the bran and add chaff and corn, the latter beginning at about a pound or less a day, until the full ration is reached. If bran and oats are not available it is quite easy to improvise in a similar manner with roots, etc., in the place of bran, gradually increasing the allowance of the oat-substitutes.

The simplest and safest changes, for variety, apart from the addition of roots and green food, can be made in the hay. The type used, clover, meadow or seeds, should always be varied from time to time, or the same kind but from different districts, or even meadows, makes a welcome change.

Feeding Ponies

From reference to the chapter on breeds, it will be seen that our native ponies are hardy little animals thriving on indifferent pasture under severe conditions. In domestication they retain this quality, unless softened by unnatural management, and can live happily at grass all the year round, with some protection against the worst weather. They do, of course, require feeding in winter and should have their ration of hay to replace the grass. Generally speaking, oats should not be fed, but a pound or two may be allowed after a hard day's work, such as hunting. Living out, they take their own exercise and are not difficult to handle, but when stabled they soon become frisky and cannot be allowed oats, or their small riders will find them too "hot" or even unmanageable. (See also page 71.)

15
Keeping horses at grass

It is well known that good grass contains all the nourishment a horse requires to keep him in health. The extent to which he is kept at grass, however, must depend upon the particular circumstances.

Polo ponies and show jumpers may be wintered out, since their work is performed in the summer, and winter is the only time they can be completely rested. From the point of view of economy, this system has little to commend it, the only saving being in bedding and a certain amount of work, but it may have to be adopted by the spare-time horseman. Animals living out during winter months need to be particularly well fed, as much of their food is used up in maintaining body heat; properly fed and with their natural coat horses will be found to be comfortably warm.

It is the practice for hunters to be turned out during the summer, when their work is finished. In their case, given suitable grazing, they will find for themselves all the food they require, but the advantages of this system are doubtful. For most of the daylight hours they will be pestered by flies and unable either to graze or rest in comfort, and in any case a month or two will be needed to get them into good, hard working condition after their "rest". In fact, to rest a *fit* horse by throwing him out of work completely for any length of time is unnecessary and unsatisfactory. It is probably an example of die-hard custom as much as a means of economising in work and expense.

A method much to be preferred, which is largely practised by riding stables, many private owners and farmers—and all those who think of their animals, as horsemen should, first, last and all the time—is that of turning out to grass at night. Not only is a certain amount of food and bedding, and some labour, saved, but the horses are far more able to enjoy their liberty when the heat of the day is past and they are spared the attention of flies.

When brought in for the day, horses benefit by being bedded-down for part of the time so that they are encouraged to rest during the heat of the day if they are not working. They will, of course, need feeding while in; three small hay feeds per day are sufficient if they are idle, but some will make one hay net last most of the day in such circumstances. Turn them out late in the afternoon and bring them in again the following morning about eight or nine o'clock—do not worry about their losing a night's sleep; horses need but little sleep, three or four hours are all they ask. It may not be generally known that a horse seldom sleeps for more than half-an-hour at a stretch, then he will get up, chew a few mouthfuls of grass, and then possibly sleep for another half hour.

Hunters can be rested and still kept in working condition with this system, if given an hour or two's steady exercise during the cooler parts of the day and allowed a "light work" ration as shown in the graph on pages 66/67. Considered economically, this does not appear to be the cheapest form of summering, but the owner is amply rewarded by the well-being of his animals.

Children's ponies are generally kept out either all the year round—and this is no hardship if suitable shelter is available against heat, flies, driving rain and cold winds, according to the time of year—or else turned out in term-time and brought in only when the children return for their holidays. Ponies of this class cannot be considered in the same way as horses; stabling and feeding produce little demons jumping out of their skins with high spirits, whilst the bitterest weather and only poor feeding find them still game and fit, but manageable and normally safe.

Remember, however, that Nature is not always perfect or kind; natural conditions are not always necessarily the best, and I am by no means advocating neglect of ponies. Careful observation is necessary to see that they have what they need to keep them in condition without "getting above themselves". It is a tragedy that, too often, ponies are bought for young children by parents without knowledge or experience of horses and are left entirely in their care. Some of the unhappy results we have all seen. I would suggest to all parents that they enrol their children with the Pony Club of the local Hunt, where they will

THE SHIRE: Largest of the heavy draught horses; descended from the war horse and the chariot horse. Similar to the Clydesdale.

"Farmer and Stockbreeder" photograph

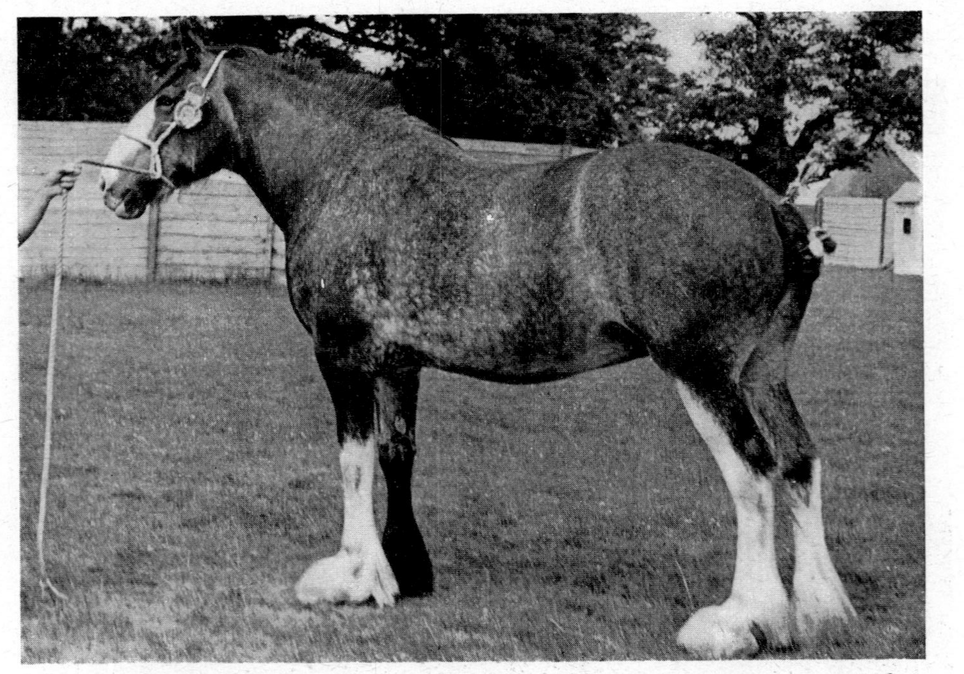

THE CLYDESDALE: The "Scottish Shire" but lighter, more active and with less feathering.

THE SUFFOLK PUNCH: Note the massive neck, which gives it its name, characteristic of the breed. Excellent for heavy agricultural work, and for crossing to produce saddle horses.

"Farmer and Stockbreeder" photograph

BRITISH PERCHERON: A hard worker of French origin, introduced into England after the 1914-18 War. Similar to the Suffolk Punch.

"Farmer and Stockbreeder" photograph

CLEVELAND BAY: Another descendant of the war horse; the state carriage horse of modern days.

YORKSHIRE COACH HORSE: A lighter relative of the Cleveland, at one time in demand for fast stage coaches.

HACKNEY HORSE: Famous in the show ring for its high smart action, but once a favourite saddle horse.

"Pony/Light Horse" photograph

THOROUGHBRED: "The whole appearance suggests speed and alertness".

THE ARAB: "Quality, gracefulness and courage combined with docility and intelligence". The foundation of the English Thoroughbred.

Photo. by courtesy of "Riding" ("Country Life")

HUNTER: A fine example of a hunter in action, jumping confidently and freely. Notice

Field Shelter.

Courtesy of Agricultural Supply Co., London

COB: An excellent saddle horse, and one that can gallop.
"Pony/Light Horse" photograph

WELSH COB: Developed from the Welsh Mountain Pony. This is the only distinct breed of cob.
"Pony/Light Horse" photograph

DALES PONY: "A miniature cart-horse"; surefooted and a great trotter.

"Pony/Light Horse" photograph

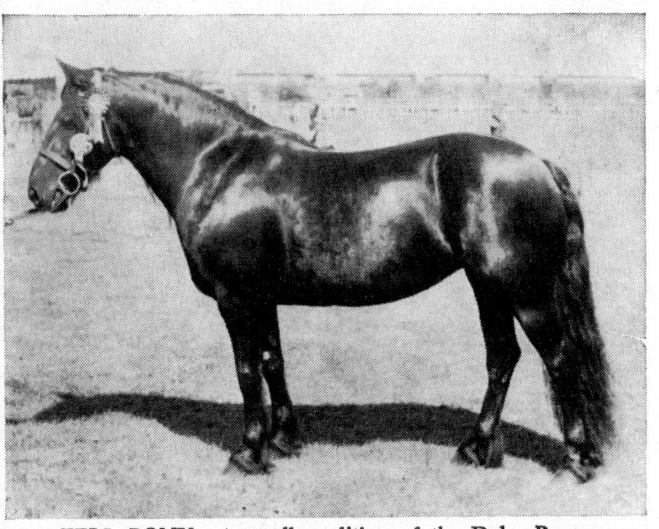

FELL PONY: A smaller edition of the Dales Pony.

"Pony/Light Horse" photograph

NEW FOREST PONY: Excellent as a children's pony or in harness

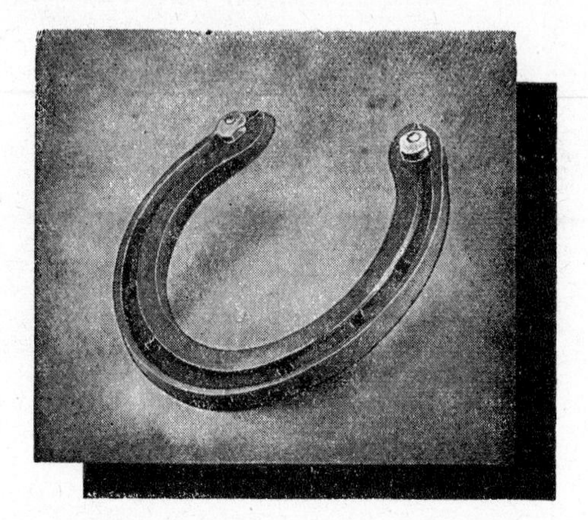

"Mordax" studs fitted to a shoe.

New and part-worn "Mordax" studs; the one on the right has had considerable wear but shows the hard "core" which makes it still effective.

EXMOOR PONY: "A little weight-carrier."
"Pony/Light Horse" photograph

HIGHLAND PONY: Gentle, intelligent, surefooted and strong.

DARTMOOR PONY: a popular children's pony.

"Pony/Light Horse" photograph

SHETLAND PONY: The smallest and longest-lived of all our ponies. Formerly used in coal mines, but now popular with children.

"Pony/Light Horse" photograph

WELSH MOUNTAIN PONY: Probably the finest of all ponies, with quality, endurance, pluck, and docility, it is ideal for children. Note the resemblance to the Arab.

"Pony/Light Horse" photograph

receive first-class instruction and guidance in riding and the care of ponies, and that both should become members of the National Pony Society and take an interest in our fine native breeds.

Feeding Value of Grass. The value of grass as a food in a normal year may be reckoned to last from May until October, and this value will depend upon the nature and extent of the grazing as well as upon the number of horses or ponies kept. A careful watch must be maintained upon the animals to see that they are doing well, or if they require supplementary feeding, as they probably will at the beginning and end of the season. If in any doubt, the horses themselves will soon settle the question; when they cease to show interest in good hay, one may be sure the grass is sufficient.

Types of Grasses. Horses do not need such rich grazing as fattening cattle, yet any muddy patch of weeds is by no means good enough. No great experience is needed to judge the suitability of grazing. It is said, with much truth, that horses do well where hedges and trees, particularly the oak and ash, flourish.

To many people, grass is just grass and as such is suitable food for horses. This is not so; many types of grasses are dismissed by farmers and horsemasters as "weeds", that is, as having no feeding value themselves and obstructing the growth of useful pasture plants and taking valuable nourishment from the soil. The best pasture grasses are those which, besides being readily grazed, last longest and are not easily stifled by weeds. Some of the most useful grasses are included in the Fescue types, and of these Meadow Fescue is outstanding, producing a first-class level pasturage. Timothy (Meadow Cat's Tail) and Cocksfoot should have their place, the former making good hay, but Cocksfoot quickly becomes coarse and is unsuitable for hay. Meadow Fox Tail, a hardy, productive grass, is good in pasture and meadow. Another plant also useful in hay, for which it is well known in the South of England, is Yellow Oat Grass, but the larger Tall Oat has a bitter taste disliked by horses.

Small-growing herbage is needed to produce a level sward by forming "bottom" or "sole" to fill in between the larger "top" grasses. For this purpose, the Rough and Smooth-stalked Meadow Grasses are excellent and liked by grazing animals. Crested Dog's Tail, found with Hard and Sheep's Fescue in sheep pasture on the Downs, is a good, nutritious grass but of little hay value, whilst the Rye Grasses, although giving valuable feed both as grazing and hay, are short-lived on anything but heavy land. Other "sole" grasses are found also in the Fescues; in addition to "Hard" and "Sheep's", there are the "Various-leaved", doing well on light, thin land, and "Creeping Fescue" on light, wet land. The soil contains nitrogen in an elementary state, and leguminous plants, such as the Clovers and Trefoils, are required to collect and turn this nitrogen into its useful form for grazing animals.

These notes on herbage plants are intended only as a guide to an interesting subject worth closer attention from horse keepers than it usually gets.

As is well known, there are types of weeds which are poisonous to horses, and an inspection should be made before turning out. Among these poisonous plants may be mentioned Hemlock and Cow-Bane, both resembling Cow Parsley which is so much relished, poison ivy, some types of privet and laurel, and of course, yew and deadly nightshade. (See "Poisoning", page 157.)

Shade and Shelter. An important point when selecting grazing (when selection is possible) is shelter from a hot sun and protection against driving rain and keen winds, which, even in summer, may be expected. Some protection is afforded by trees and hedges, which should be available on any grazing.

Everyone who has seen horses at grass during the summer will have noticed the annoyance caused by flies, and so persistent are these pests at times that during the day horses are allowed little opportunity of grazing, which explains why a run at grass in hot weather, far from acting as the intended rest and pick-me-up, frequently leads to loss of flesh. Unfortunately, it is in the shade of trees and bushes that flies usually swarm most viciously, driving the distracted animals out again into the glare of the sun, where they stand stamping, shaking their heads and swishing their tails in an effort to get rid of their tormentors. No really effective anti-fly lotion has yet been made.

The provision of a sheltering building is not only desirable but necessary, unless the method described on page 88 is adopted. It need not be an elaborate structure so long as it is firmly erected and unlikely to suffer or cause damage in high winds. All that is needed is an open-fronted shelter, similar to that shown in the middle of the book, placed in a position to keep out the rays of the sun during the greater part of the day, where there will be peace from flies and, when necessary, protection from the weather. A simple field shelter of this kind can be easily and cheaply built of feather-edge boarding on stout timbers sunk firmly in the ground, the sunken parts being well tarred; the dimensions should be not less than those of a loose-box for each horse. Do not be disappointed if you find this shelter seldom used; it is there if needed, and it will be if flies become too troublesome or the wind too keen. It is also a useful place for feeding in the winter, and horses soon appreciate the little extra comfort it gives them.

A docked horse suffers even greater torments from flies than does his more fortunate companion, being unable to protect those parts of his body not provided by Nature with twitching "fly-muscles", except with his head. Nor can he expect his companion with a tail to keep the flies from his face by standing head-to-tail with him, since he is unable to return the favour. It is, of course, cruelty to turn out such an animal in "fly weather". The reasons given for docking were unconvincing: For Cobs and Hackneys it was said to be a question of appearance, but it was probably merely bowing to the fashion. Compare the docked hunter depicted in an old print with the hunter of to-day; which gains in appearance? For draught horses it was said to be a question of safety, to prevent the tail being caught up in the harness. Here it was perhaps only laziness; to groom a tail well takes time, so, off with his tail. Many farmers supply the answer by tying up tails before putting their horses in the shafts—but farmers are notoriously level-headed. I cannot remember, either, seeing draught horses in the Army minus their tails, and one could hardly argue that the Service in those days was governed by sentimentalists! Nature is not in the habit of doing things without reason, and she had good reason for supplying tails as "standard fittings"; the "Docking and Nicking" Bill was therefore to be welcomed.

Fences, Gates, etc. Having satisfied yourself as to the

suitability of the paddock, there are still other points calling for attention.

The ground, fences and hedges should be regularly inspected for dangerous objects; it is amazing what peculiar things find resting places in paddocks which adjoin roads or are situated in suburban areas. Broken bottles, large flints, bricks and other possible causes of injury seem to grow overnight, while hedges and fences only too frequently bristle with barbed wire entanglements. Mole hills, rabbit stops and ant heaps should be levelled off, as they are a menace to galloping horses.

Fences and gates must be secure and escape-proof. You may have the finest pasture, yet to most animals there is always an irresistible attraction in your neighbour's. As to the kind of fencing, you will need no warning against that invention of the devil (I usually call it something stronger)—barbed wire, but nearly as dangerous are low, sharp-pointed chestnut palings and spiked iron railings. "Posts and Rails" make the best fencing, perhaps, but any type can be used so long as it conforms to certain standards: it must be sufficiently high to discourage jumping out (usually five feet is ample); strong enough to withstand high winds or the pressure of horses rubbing against it; free from gaps through which a nimble and cunning pony could squeeze; and it must, as already mentioned, present no pointed or sharp portions even remotely capable of inflicting injury. You probably know that the owner of an animal found straying on the highway may be fined, the animal impounded or, sometimes, sold.

Time and trouble spent on fences and gates in the first place are time and trouble saved later, as probably fifty per cent of the injuries to horses at grass can be traced to neglect in these items. If it is possible to adopt a form of fencing which will protect the animal from the attentions and mistaken kindnesses of passers-by, your mind will be relieved of much worry. Many a young horse has been spoilt in temper by tit-bits and unintentional teasing at the fence, and many a horse has suffered or even died from eating unsuitable plants fed to him by well-meaning but ignorant animal-lovers. It is characteristic of most horses that they will accept from the hand that which they would not otherwise eat.

Water. Finally, ensure a constant supply of fresh, clean

water. If a natural supply is at hand, in the form of a stream or pond, make certain it is suitable. A stream is obviously to be preferred to any other source, so long as it is unpolluted at any point either in or before reaching the paddock, but stagnant ponds or pools are to be avoided and should be fenced off. For an artificial supply, try to secure a large, easily-cleaned receptacle capable of being quickly filled without undue labour. Failing a proper drinking trough, a time-expired enamelled bath is excellent, being of adequate capacity even for several horses—a horse drinks from eight to fifteen gallons a day—and easily cleaned. The green slime that forms in any water trough is harmless in itself but can harbour injurious germs and parasites and should not be allowed to remain. Do not imagine, because a horse is at grass, from which he certainly obtains some moisture, that water is in any degree less necessary than in the stable. Summer or winter, wet or fine, ample, pure water *must* be available or condition will suffer.

Management at Grass

Care of Pasture. Grass is a valuable crop, and as such is to be carefully tended, more especially as the acreage of both pasture and meadowland is diminishing annually owing to commercial and residential development. Of what is known as "first-class", or cattle-fattening pasture, there is already little left in this country and the amount of second-class pasture, or ordinary grazing, is tragically small.

In ideal circumstances, particularly when horses live out all the year round, there will be a change of grazing available. In this connection two small paddocks are better than a single large one, as one may be rested while the other is in use, and it is worth while dividing a large field into two for this reason. Land quickly becomes "horse-sick", the growth of herbage coarse and unpalatable, and before long the pasture is useless as such. When circumstances permit, the resting paddock will be improved by chain-harrowing and rolling towards the end of the winter or in the spring. Harrowing distributes the droppings evenly over the surface, pulls out moss and matted growths of grass and allows air to enter the soil. It is bad practice to leave dung undisturbed, as it destroys for a time the plants beneath and that part becomes ringed with rank, dark grass and weeds. In a small paddock, or when harrowing is out of the question, dung should be collected regularly and removed, or at least frequently scattered with a fork. Rolling consolidates and presses the soil around the roots of plants after disturbance by grazing and frost.

Horses will eat right down the best grass and leave the rest, so that patches of long, coarse stuff result. These must be systematically cut down, as must also thistles and other weeds. Cattle will be found very helpful here, as they will browse grass that horses miss.

A common system is to take a crop of hay from the resting paddock, and although this is not considered the best practice since, it is said, land kept solely for grazing produces the most suitable grass for this purpose, the rule applying similarly to land kept for hay alone, yet its advantages may often outweigh its disadvantages. On the other hand, the succulent and nourishing spring grass should not be sacrificed unnecessarily for a small crop of possibly inferior hay. The question of "to hay or not to hay" can only be decided by the horse-owner concerned, having regard to his particular circumstances and according to whether winter hay, whatever its quality, is likely to be more valuable than summer grass.

The use of top dressing must be regulated according to the nature of the soil, but most grazing land is improved by dressings of lime, kainit, or basic slag.

Feeding. It has already been said that normally grass supplies sufficient keep from May until October, and that the horse's reactions towards dry feeds can be taken as a guide to his requirements in the way of supplementary feeding. Given, then, reasonable grazing and a good season, there is not much need to worry about anything but winter feeding for a horse not brought in during the day and doing little or no work. Lack of grass in winter calls for a supply of hay to make good the deficiency in bulk, and a "maintenance ration" of the best hay procurable should be given—as shown in the graph on pages 66/67—preferably divided into two feeds and given in hay nets. As well, grain may be needed to keep up the body temperature, and this should be fed in the form of crushed oats (or a substitute) at the "light work" rate, mixed with a couple of handfuls of chaff in two feeds. When possible, a pound or two of beans or peas could be usefully included —see page 76.

Working. It will be readily appreciated that a grass-fed horse cannot be expected to perform the same amount or type of work as a corn-fed one; fast work should not be asked of him. A working horse should be given a small corn feed on his return, say 3 lbs. of oats with two double handfuls of chaff; when there is a lack of grass he must, of course, receive the appropriate ration according to his size and work.

Being unclipped, there is more likelihood of the animal returning from work hot and sweating, even with the greatest consideration on the part of the rider or driver, and on no account should he be unsaddled or unharnessed and turned loose without first being thoroughly dried and cooled. Failure to observe this elementary precaution may quite easily lead to serious consequences.

The grooming of a horse living out is best kept to the minimum necessary for appearance, since the grease and long hair in the coat are required for warmth and "water-proofing".

General Hints. The process of changing from stable to grass feeding should be gradual to avoid gorging and the harmful effects of a sudden change in diet.

When being turned out into a field for the first few times, it is to be expected that some excitement and impatience will be shown—a few bucks and kicks will be displayed as soon as the horse is free. To safeguard yourself, face him towards the gate while taking off his head-collar, then stand clear. Remember, too, when horses are allowed to pass through a gate by themselves, the gate must be *wide open,* otherwise, in the rush and excitement, serious injuries are possible from knocks and scrapes.

Before horses are finally left at grass for any length of time, unless they are still to be worked regularly, reduce the chances of injuries to each other from kicks by having the hind shoes removed. To prevent splitting of the hoof, if the fore-shoes are also removed, have the lower margin of the wall bevelled or the feet shod in front with grass tips —but in the latter case heed the warning on page 103. Monthly attention by the farrier will still be necessary.

Every day the animals must be examined for any injuries or other troubles. The teeth, also, may need inspection at intervals; the tables of the cheek teeth are not worn to any extent by chewing grass, and the edges may become very sharp.

For the less hardy breeds, and those which grow but little coat in the winter—Thoroughbreds particularly—the "All-Weather" or "New Zealand" waterproof rugs are useful. These rugs, which are made to allow freedom of movement and to right themselves after rolling, are perfectly safe, all being fitted with leg straps or fillet strings to keep them in place. It is very important that they should be of correct size and fitting, and that the leg straps should be properly adjusted so that there is no possibility of either chafing of the legs or of a leg being caught up. Watch regularly, also, for any chafing around the shoulders. The makers will supply full directions regarding the use and fitting of their own rugs. (See also Chapter 9.)

Horses are gregarious animals and appreciate companions, so try to provide yours with one, even if only a donkey.

16
The foot and shoeing

If the truth of the old saying, "No foot, no horse", is realised, a good farrier must be considered as one of the best friends of the horse keeper. An incompetent farrier can, in time, ruin the feet and render a valuable horse useless, but the modern, qualified shoeing-smith is a highly-skilled specialist. He had made a comprehensive study of his art, including not only the actual practice of shoeing, but also its relation with the anatomy of the foot and leg, a subject in which he is well versed. He can rectify many cases of deformity, poor action, etc., and on such matters his advice should always be sought.

At the same time, it is well for the horse keeper to be conversant with the interesting, elementary principles of shoeing, and to have some knowledge of the structure of the foot and the functions of its various parts.

Construction of the Foot

The foot is constructed of an inner "core" of bones, surrounded by continuous fleshy parts (collectively known as the "Pododerm", or, commonly, the "quick"). These fleshy parts are responsible for their own corresponding horny structures in the protective outer casing, the hoof. The bones involved are, the lower portion of the Coronet Bone (short pastern), the Coffin or Pedal Bone, which gives the hoof its shape, and the Navicular Bone, situated between the wings of the Pedal Bone. The sensitive, or fleshy parts, are considered as they occur in the following sections. These parts are served by numerous blood-vessels, which explains why even a small wound here bleeds profusely. The horny hoof comprises the wall, sole and frog.

The Wall. As its name implies, this is the part of the hard, horny, insensitive casing seen when the foot is flat upon the ground. It can be compared with our own nails, and, like them, is always growing. Nourishment for its growth is derived from the Coronary Cushion or Band, a

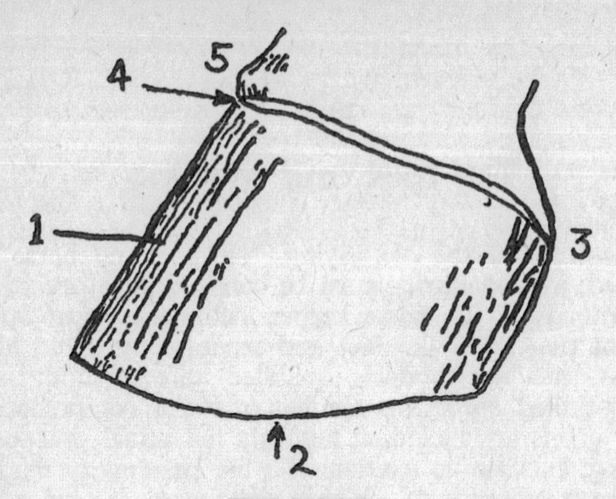

THE HOOF

1. Wall
2. Sole
3. Bulbs of Heels
4. Frog Band
5. Coronary Cushion

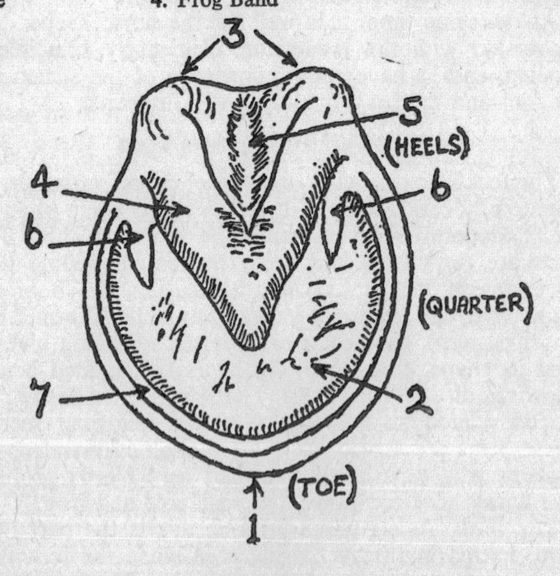

THE HOOF

1. Ground Surface of Wall
2. Sole
3. Bulbs of Heels
4. Frog
5. Cleft of Frog
6. Bars
7. White Line

fleshy structure carried at the upper part of the wall and seen as a bulge extending round the Coronet. Toughness and some flexibility are imparted by the presence of a certain amount of water in the horn, evaporation being prevented by a thin layer of hard "varnish", the Periople. The Periople is secreted from the Perioplic Band, a fleshy ring around the top of the hoof, above the Coronary Cushion, noticeable as a white band when the foot is wet.

The parts of the wall are known as the toe, quarters, (that is, the sides) and heels. The toe is the thickest and highest part, the wall gradually becoming thinner and shorter towards the heels, turning inwards here as the "Bars". The "Angle of the heels" formed by the Bars is also known as the "seat of corn". The ground surface of the wall, which carries the shoe, is called the "bearing surface".

An unshod horse wears away the growth of horn naturally, but it can be seen that a shod foot needs periodic shortening—usually every three or four weeks. Neglect of this attention means an overgrown foot, which, by natural spreading, becomes too large for the shoe and breaks away at the nail holes or overlaps the shoe, with consequent lameness. Sometimes, when the horn is very sound, a well put on shoe acts as an iron band and prevents *outward* growth, particularly at the heels, causing long, narrow feet with pointed toes—for which the farrier is often subsequently blamed. Even unshod, at grass, the feet may need trimming, since some grow more rapidly than others, and on soft ground, especially damp soils, growth is encouraged. There have been many cases of old or lame horses turned out unshod, whose feet have grown to such a length, through neglect, that they have had to be mercifully destroyed.

The Sole. The outer, horny sole grows from the sensitive or fleshy sole covering the under part of the pedal bone, and should be concave from the ground surface. Between the wall and the sole is the "white line", a ring of soft horn, the edge of which is visible at the ground surface. The white line allows expansion of the sole when weight is put upon it, and to the farrier indicates the thickness of the wall and the nail-room available.

As a general rule no paring of the sole is necessary at shoeing, since it flakes away naturally during growth. It used to be the custom to pare the sole until it was "springy" and could be pressed inwards; eventually it was proved that only harm resulted from the practice, which has now ceased as such. However, there are cases where the sole does *not* flake away and must be pared; the skilled farrier recognises the condition and proceeds accordingly. Failure to pare the sole on such occasions may allow the feet to become very long and necessitate extra cutting eventually.

The Frog. If the foot is held up, the frog can be seen as a rubbery, triangular piece of horn projecting below the level of the sole. Growing from the sensitive or fleshy frog, which covers the "Plantar Cushion" situated inside the hoof, it is very elastic and acts as a shock-absorber and non-slip device. It has another function, frequently overlooked, that of assisting in the circulation of the blood supply in the foot when blood-vessels become flattened against the wall by expansion of the structures under pressure. The Plantar Cushion, extending from the rearmost portion of the foot (the bulbs of the heels) to the Pedal Bone, is of very elastic, fibrous tissue resembling the frog in shape, which it assists as a shock-absorber. The comprehensive provision in this region against concussion is necessary because the heels meet the ground before the toe, and the frog and its associated structures must bear the first shock.

The frog, then, to carry out its functions, must always make contact with the ground and should therefore never be pared except for the removal of any "rags". Extra growth is worn away by the friction of contact with the ground and by the forming of ragged portions. Although subjected to so much weight, shock and wear, the frog is rarely injured, owing to its toughness and elasticity, but it may suffer cuts from glass, sharp and jagged stones and picked-up foreign bodies (hence the need to examine feet after work).

Shoeing

Materials. Mild steel is normally used for making shoes, although other materials, notably rubber, have been tried with the object of reducing concussion and providing better grip on slippery surfaces.

As a general rule, the shoe should be no thicker than

necessary for the type of work, but should be sufficient to give about four weeks' normal wear.

In modern practice, the farrier buys his steel in bars of suitable sections, from which he cuts required lengths to make the shoes, or he may buy machine-made shoes of various sizes. As might be expected, the hand-made article is superior to the machine-made one, and the latter must be finished by hand. The holes are pitched at a sharper angle than is possible with a machine, enabling the farrier to get better position and hold for his nails. The system of welding two old shoes together and working them to make one new one produced a shoe of great toughness, owing to the extra hammering necessary. This system is seldom seen to-day for typically modern reasons—expensive and poor quality fuel and increased labour costs.

The Shoe: Terms and Parts

Cover. This refers to the width of the metal and is frequently interchangeable with—

Web. Although "web" may be loosely employed with the same meaning as "cover", it strictly includes also the thickness of the material, that is, the whole cubic area of metal.

Toe and Heel. No explanation of these terms is needed.

Branch. The complete side of the shoe from toe to heel, corresponding to the "quarter" in the foot.

Quarter. The part of the branch between the toe and heel. Thus there are two branches in each shoe.

Bearing or Foot Surface. The surface of the shoe on which the foot rests.

Fullering. A fullered shoe is grooved in the ground surface, for about half its depth, either all round or for the nail holes only. The intention is to provide increased grip, and, particularly in heavy machine-made shoes, for easier piercing of nail holes. It cannot, as sometimes claimed, make the shoe lighter since no metal is actually *removed* in fullering. Slipping is prevented, to some extent, not only by the edges of the fullering, but more by the small stones, grit, etc., which collect in the groove.

Calkins and Wedges. A calkin is a projection at the heel of the hind shoe, made by turning a small piece of the metal downwards to give better foothold, and is found especially useful when going downhill on slippery grass. It may be on both, or on the outer heel only, and in the latter case the inside heel must be brought to a similar level by thickening, known as a "wedge heel". It must be remembered that calkins soon wear down and become ineffective.

Clips. These are small triangular pieces drawn from the outer edge of the shoe, fitting into shallow "beds" or nicks cut out in the wall of the hoof. Their object is to prevent movement of the shoe backwards or sideways. They should be no larger than necessary for the size of shoe, a short clip with a good base being stronger than a long, thin one, and they may be placed at the toe or at each quarter. On the fore-shoe a toe clip is used, and whilst many farriers treat the hind-shoe similarly, quarter clips instead slightly lessen the risk of over-reaching, that is, striking the heel or back tendon of the forefoot with the toe of the hind. In a horse that brushes (strikes one foot against the opposite fetlock when moving) it is often advisable to have one toe clip and one at the outside quarter to stop the shoe moving to the inside of the foot. In many saddle horses they can be dispensed with altogether—see "Set-up Toe"—and often are in racehorses.

Types of Shoes

Plain Shoe. This is a shoe with a flat ground surface, the holes being "plain stamped", that is, without fullering.

Flat Shoe. "Flat" refers to the foot surface of the shoe, which, in this case, covers the bearing surface of the wall, the white line and a small portion of the sole and bars.

Seated Shoe. In a seated shoe, the bearing surface is bevelled or hollowed out at the inner edge so that it makes little or no contact with the sole. As has been seen in "The Construction of the Foot", page 97, the sole is normally slightly concave and therefore this precaution is only necessary for feet that are flat or have a dropped sole. (The farrier often refers to a flat foot as "fleshy".) There is usually no objection to the sole taking some bearing, which will not cause lameness, and is, in fact, often recommended. Disadvantages of a seated shoe are that it is more likely to be loosened by suction in deep going, and dirt collects in the seating.

Concave Shoe. A concave shoe is ground-seated, that is, bevelled or hollowed out at the inside edge of the ground surface, making this narrower than the bearing surface. This pattern is common for saddle horses, particularly hunters, for which it is useful as it is less likely to be sucked off in deep, holding ground, and is lighter than an ordinary shoe.

Rodway Shoe. This is a shoe with double fullering, the second groove, on the inner side, not being pierced with nail holes. There does not seem to be much advantage in this pattern except that it may give slightly better foot-hold, for the same reasons as single fullering. Similarly, it cannot be lighter than a plain shoe. Formerly popular for carriage horses, it is now seldom seen.

Set-up and Rolled Toe. There is little difference between these two and they may therefore be considered together. At the toe, half the width of the web in the foreshoe is bent up, usually at an angle of about 22 degrees; no clip is used, but the wall of the foot must be rasped back at this part for reception of the turned-up toe. Although sometimes the hind shoe is not set-up or rolled, but has clips at the sides, there is a good case for rolling the toe. This part wears before any other, so that if it is rolled, the whole shoe has a longer life and may therefore be made thinner and lighter, giving increased frog pressure with consequent reduction of concussion and risk of slipping. Since stumbling is frequently the result of putting the toe down first, if the shoe is rolled and shortened at the toe there is less chance of its catching as the heel comes to the ground. For these reasons it seems that many cases of lameness would be avoided by the use of rolled toes, and certainly the ideal requirements are more nearly approached—a light shoe giving sufficient wear for three to four weeks and allowing the frog to function.

Grass Tips. These are half-shoes, designed to protect the horn from splitting at the toe. Although intended for horses at grass, they may be useful for ponies doing little work on hard surfaces, or for youngsters on leading exercise. In these cases, a watch must be kept on the feet to see that no excessive wear is being imposed upon the unshod parts. In all instances they must be inspected regularly for looseness, and *removed every four weeks* to rectify uneven growth of the ground surface of the wall. Failure to do so upsets the balance of the foot and imposes strain on the tendons. To fit correctly, the ground surface of the tip and the bare portion of the wall must be level, which necessitates the branches tapering towards the ends. Four nails are required for fixing.

Shoes for Various Types of Horses

Hunters and Hacks. On account of the similarity of their work, the same pattern of shoe is usually appropriate. For these horses, provision has to be made to counteract the suction of heavy going covered at fast paces, and both fore and hind shoes should therefore have a fullered, concave ground surface. The inner branches must follow the line of the wall exactly, or even be set slightly under to avoid brushing.

The front shoe is usually clipped at the toe, and should be rolled slightly as a precaution against stumbling, but it is suggested again that the advantages of the real set-up toe should not be overlooked. To prevent the heels being trodden on and the shoe pulled off by the hind toe, at the gallop, these should not extend beyond the wall of the foot at the back, and many farriers make them a fraction of an inch shorter than the wall. The heels are also bevelled down to match the angle of the heels of the foot.

There are several ways of treating the hind shoes. Toe clips, although often used, are not recommended. If clips are employed, it is better to place them each side of the toe, which should be "squared off" or even "set back" a little, to avoid over-reaching or "forging" at fast paces in deep ground. ("Forging" is striking the front shoe with the toe of the hind, hence the descriptive terms "clicking" and "clacking", also applied.) Instead of clips, a set-up toe has obvious advantages. The branches need not be shortened, as in the fore-shoe, and, for better grip, the outer heel is sometimes fitted with a small calkin, the inner branch having a wedge heel. Calkins are unnecessary for hacks, as galloping on deep ground can be avoided.

Weights vary from 4 to 5 lbs. per set; ponies proportionately according to their size, from about 2½ lbs. for 12 hands in height.

Carriage-type Horses. Since their work is on roads, at slow paces, a heavier shoe can be used, but provision against slipping is necessary, and for this purpose calkins are fitted on the hind shoes. Rodways were commonly employed when carriage horses were numerous. The practice now for this type is usually fullered shoes in front and plain shoes behind, though the hind shoes also are sometimes fullered.

The weight of a set of shoes is about 4 to 6 lbs. for lighter animals and up to about 8 lbs. for heavier horses and vanners.

Draught Horses. The type of horse to be provided for is one doing slow, often heavy work, which calls for a shoe giving good foothold, particularly when hauling heavy loads. Therefore, large calkins are made on the heels of the hind shoes, which may be wide fitting with the same object, especially as brushing is unlikely at their speeds. To increase foothold, toe pieces may be added—a strip of metal welded on slightly behind the toe. Flat shoes are used, plain when hand-made, but fullered when machine-made, on account of the thickness of the web.

A set will weigh anything up to 20 lbs.

Racehorses. For these, two patterns are in use; a light, fullered, concave shoe of mild steel for training, and a fullered, concave "plate", generally of aluminium, for racing.

Training shoes weigh about 1½ lbs. per set, and racing plates ½ to 1 lb. per set.

Preparing the Foot. As was seen in the description of the construction of the foot, all that is necessary is to remove the growth that has taken place in the wall since the last shoeing. This is done with the "toeing knife" (or with the pincer-like "hoof cutters" in the case of unshod youngsters objecting to this, which necessitates the use of the hammer). The wall is then levelled with the rasp, and beds for the clips cut in the horn either with the same knife or with the curved "drawing knife".

Fitting the Shoe. The first principle of good shoeing is that the shoe must be made to fit the foot. It is not to be expected that at first trial the shoe will be found to be exactly right; it must be worked until it is. But the foot must not be cut and rasped to make a good fit—one would hardly agree to a shoemaker removing a slice of one's big toe to make the foot suitable for his shoe.

The usual method of fitting is by "hot shoeing". The shoe is heated in the fire and then applied to the bearing surface of the wall; by the slight charring of the horn, the farrier judges the fit of the shoe, the size, shape and bearing. If the bearing is level, the hot shoe will mark the horn *evenly* all round, indicating that the foot and shoe meet each other correctly at all points, leaving no "daylight" anywhere. To the uninitiated, hot shoeing with its smoke and smell of burning hoof appears to be a painful process; it is not, of course, nor is the driving of nails through the wall, since the horn is insensitive. On the other hand, the animal can feel even a light touch here, owing to the generous distribution of nerves in the sensitive structures and their close contact with the insensitive parts.

Another method is "cold shoeing", much used in the Army on service, due to the impossibility of transporting forges, etc., and also employed to a great extent in civilian life when circumstances dictate. This calls for greater skill and a keener eye, but a competent shoeing-smith produces perfectly satisfactory results.

If there is sufficient wear left in the old shoes, these may be used again, after the excess horn has been pared away, when the process is known as "removes".

Nailing. It will be noticed that the number of nail holes may differ in various sets of shoes. The machine-made ones often have more than the hand-made, but that does not mean they all have to be used; their purpose is to allow the farrier some choice in placing his nails. The least number necessary to keep the shoe in position is the rule, and seven are commonly used, three at the inside quarter, four at the outside. Since the shoe must be securely held throughout its life, the nail-heads are so designed that they do not wear down before the shoe. To achieve this, the "stamp", the tool with which the holes are punched, is wedge-shaped like the nail heads; thus holes and nails make a firm joint throughout the wear of the shoe. A "pritchel" is finally used to open the hole sufficiently at the ground surface for the nail to pass through.

Driving the nails correctly calls for skill, experience and a keen eye. The white line, as previously shown, is an indication of the thickness of the wall and therefore of the height at which the points of the nails must emerge. At too sharp an angle they penetrate the wall too low and do not obtain a good hold, being liable to break away the horn at the edge. Driven too high, their shanks come closer to the fleshy lining of the wall than safety permits, and may bruise it (a "press" or "bind"), or the points may pierce this sensitive structure, causing a "prick". It may be the holes are badly placed in the shoe, either too near the outer edge in the first fault, known as "fine stamping" or too near the inner edge in the second, known as "coarse stamping". Another reason for these faults is more frequently to be found in the thinness of the wall—some horses have walls "as thin as tissue paper", so that it is a matter of surprise, not that they are pricked, but that it happens so rarely. No farrier pricks a foot purposely, and very few do so from negligence, but even with the greatest care sometimes the point of a nail turns inwards when being driven. Due to the difference in the slope of the wall, nails at the heel are usually driven slightly lower than at the toe.

Clenching. As each nail comes through the wall, its point is immediately twisted off with the claws of the driving hammer to avoid injury if the horse makes a sudden, unexpected movement. When all nails in one shoe have been driven, the farrier places the closed jaws of his pincers against each stub, or broken end, while hammering the head of the nail home. This turns over and forms the "clenches", which he completes by hammering flat into the wall and smoothing over with the rasp. Here it will be noticed that he does not, or should not, rasp above the clenches; to do so would be pointless and harmful, and remove some of the periople unnecessarily.

Clips. When preparing the foot, small shallow beds were cut in the wall in appropriate positions for the reception of clips, which are now hammered in flat against the wall. Excessive hammering of the clips is one of the causes of "Seedy Toe" (see page 147).

Finishing. The final touch is to run a corner of the rasp around the edge of the wall where it meets the shoe to remove any small shreds of horn and bevel the wall slightly to prevent splitting. Note that only one or two quick strokes are required, and only at the *edge* of the wall. Excessive rasping down the lower part indicates that the toe of the shoe is too short and the foot is being "dumped" to fit. Dumping removes some of the protective periople and leads to brittleness of the horn, as did the old practice of sandpapering around and above the nails. Probably it will make a neat-looking finish, especially with a tasteful coating of hoof-oil, but good shoeing needs no beautifying and the neatest effect does not mean the best workmanship.

Non-Slip Shoeing

In winter extra precautions against slipping may be necessary, at least for horses working on icy roads, and there is a choice of several methods:

Roughing. Although the term "roughing" is generally loosely applied to all anti-slipping devices, apart from special patent methods mentioned later in this chapter, it strictly refers to a particular modification of the shoes themselves. The shoes are removed, and if calkins are not already present these are formed by turning down the heels. They are then sharpened to a chisel edge, the one at the outer heel lying across the shoe, the other pointing forward. Occasionally, for heavy draught horses on road work, sharpened wedges are also made at the toe, either from existing toe pieces or by welding on "sharps". Although an effective way, the need for removing the shoes is a disadvantage, especially as the wedges soon become blunt and involve further removal and sharpening. This method is rarely used to-day.

Frost Nails. These sharp hard-headed nails are fitted in place of ordinary nails at the heels, and sometimes toes; or they may be used additionally at the heels on specially wide-fitting shoes, when their shanks are turned over to secure them. They are effective but soon become worn.

Frost or Screw Cogs. These are preferable to frost nails and are easily removed at night, by "taps" or keys, to prevent injury to the horse. They are screwed into specially provided holes in each heel and sometimes also in each toe. When removed, their places should be taken by "blanks" or blunt cogs, to preserve the thread of the holes and prevent burring over of the edges. Various shaped heads are made, and when the chisel-edge type is used, they should lie in the positions described under "Roughing".

The foregoing have disadvantages and consequently have been superseded.

"Mordax" Studs. These, of which many sizes are supplied

in tapered, screw and plug types, are designed for easy fitting, to obviate rapid wear and to remain in the shoes until the latter are worn out, and have been proved an excellent non-slipping device. The weight of the horse makes the hard centre pin of the stud sink into the surface thus arresting any slip without jarring. (See illustration in centre of book.)

In fitting, the shoes are drilled or punched, while hot, at selected positions with holes which are then tapered by means of the special punch provided. When the shoes have cooled, the studs are inserted and driven down up to their shoulders, and if additional security is desired, may then be cold-riveted slightly at the back. To remove, the studs are punched out when the horse is re-shod.

Long wear has been obtained by forming the centre of the stud of exceptionally hard metal, and they are guaranteed for a minimum of 350 miles hacking and hunting, and 250 miles for light draught horses, under normal conditions.

It is usual to fit one in each heel, that is, eight per set of shoes, and the makers advise against their use in the front toes for riding horses. For a horse inclined to slip on the hind feet, many people find a stud on the outside heel of the shoe very effective, the inside heel being raised to preserve the level.

Mordax "Nails" can be used in place of the studs for horses of a lighter type. One or two nails in each shoe are sufficient to safeguard horse and rider.

"Gragrip" Method of Shoeing

Ordinary shoeing is a necessary evil which, by raising the frog out of operation, prevents its efficient functioning as a shock-absorber and non-slip device, particularly on hard roads. The "Gragrip" method has been recommended by some veterinary experts as neutralising these ill-effects by restoring to the foot Nature's even weight-bearing surface. It avoids lameness caused by constant work on hard roads, without affecting the natural gait. The method is also suitable for all types, from heavy draught to racehorses, and is not restricted to road work.

"Gragrips" consist of a thin flexible steel bridge with a rubber pad at the ground surface, the steel place cracking the first time weight is placed upon it, thus maintaining the greatest possible flexibility. There is no continuous pressure against the frog, which is allowed to descend and bear upon the steel bridge each time the foot comes to the ground, imitating the action intended by Nature. The foot makes no injurious contact with the rubber, and dirt cannot collect beneath the plate; at the same time the major portion of the foot is left open.

Fitting. "Gragrips" are made in four thicknesses, ¼ inch, ⅜ inch, ½ inch and ⅝ inch, for all sizes of shoes, fore or hind, and are easily fitted by the farrier. The steel bridge is riveted to the shoe before nailing on, and correct fitting in accordance with the makers' instructions is important. The walls and frog must first be level, as in the natural state, and the bridge must lie in a straight line across the heels, the rubber—of shoe thickness only, for a normal foot—touching each side of the shoe. To obtain level bearing, paring of the frog is not necessary. With a prominent frog, this can be achieved by using "Gragrips" thinner than the shoes (e.g. ⅜ inch on ½ inch shoes) or by thickening the heels of the shoes. With a shrunken frog, bearing can be adjusted by using thicker "Gragrips" (e.g. ⅝ inch

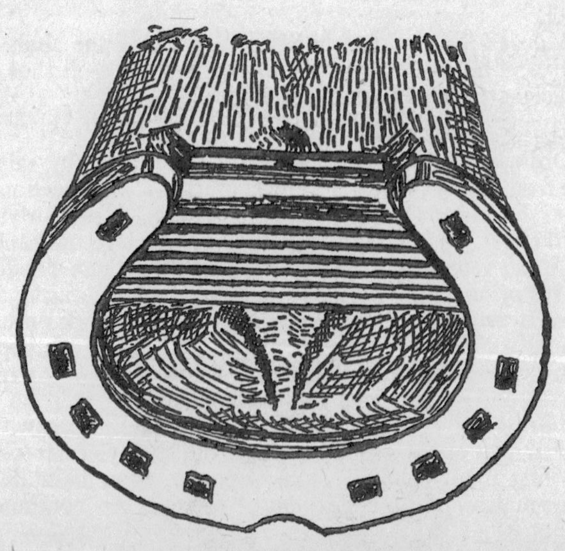

The "Gragrip" Flexible Steel Bridge special method of shoeing.

on ½ inch) or by thinning the heels of the shoes; continuous shoeing in this way develops a strong, healthy frog.

When used on horses doing little road work, the shoes and "Gragrips" may not be worn out after a month. Removes are then carried out in the normal way, restoring wall and frog level and replacing the shoes complete with their fittings. The same process can be repeated after a further month if sufficient wear still remains. Were the shoes not removed at these intervals, the growth of wall would lower the "Gragrips" out of frog contact and render them ineffective.

Under normal conditions this method of shoeing has a life of from 300 miles upwards, according to the type of horse. It is very rarely used nowadays as ordinary shoeing is perfectly satisfactory.

There is, however, a new development called the "Tad-shoe". This is made of plastic and is of traditional design. It is fixed by nails driven through metal inserts which can be placed in any desired position in the track of the shoe. It is stressed that this is not a "do it yourself" shoe and has to be fitted by a farrier.

There has been some press comment on "Do-it-yourself" shoes which can be fitted by the owner. This method has not come up to expectations, and is not to be recommended. It is risky for the horse and may cause painful (and expensive) damage. The services of an experienced farrier should always be used.

17
Bridles, saddles and harness

Riding Bridles. Since the purpose of a bridle is to hold the bit in the horse's mouth, the essential parts are the bit headstall, which passes over the head, and its cheek pieces with which it is connected to the bit. The cheek pieces are usually stitched at the bit, for the sake of neatness, but buckles or studs have advantages which, in my opinion, far outweigh any objection to their alleged clumsiness; the whole can be taken to pieces at any time for cleaning, or for changing or renewing any part—this advantage is always forcibly brought home when leather breaks.

The headstall is prevented from slipping forward by the throatlash, which forms part of it and passes around the throat to buckle on the near side. Backward movement is prevented by the browband, which crosses the forehead and has loops at either end through which the headstall passes.

A noseband is found on most bridles; this can usually be dispensed with, it being a matter of opinion whether or not it improves appearance, and much depends on the shape of the head. There may be cases, however, when a *tight* noseband gives better control with a difficult horse. It is held in position by a strap passing through the browband loops and over the poll (under the headstall) to buckle on the near side. Adjustment of the noseband itself is by a buckle under the jaw.

Bits. We are told there is a key to the mouth of every horse; this is true, but generally the real key is in the hands of the rider, driver or breaker. It is when this key has been "lost" that we have to seek one in the bit. However, horses vary, and the type of bit which will suit one will not suit another; it is usual to try first the snaffle, and if this is found unsuitable—either for control or "balance"—to progress to the double bridle or the Pelham.

The Snaffle. The common form of snaffle is one with a jointed mouthpiece, either plain or the less mild twisted,

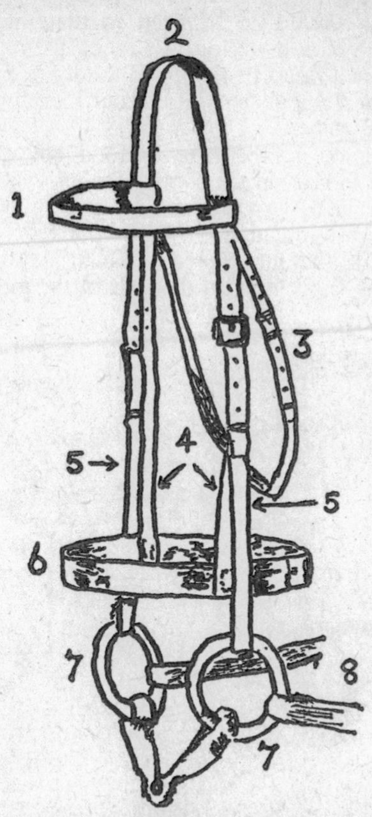

PLAIN JOINTED SNAFFLE

1. Browband
2. Crown Piece or Head Piece
3. Throatlash
4. Support or Cheek Piece of Noseband
5. Cheek Strap of Bit Headstall
6. Noseband
7. Snaffle Rings
8. Snaffle Reins

with large flat rings either end. Jointed snaffles allow freedom for the tongue but are capable of a painful nutcracker effect on the corners of the mouth. The straight bar snaffle, with the mouthpiece in one complete straight piece of metal, is little seen; it does not allow the same tongue freedom but is without the nutcracker effect of the jointed variety.

Snaffle bits should be adjusted so that they touch the corners of the mouth without wrinkling them.

The Double Bridle. In this form there are two bits: the bridoon or snaffle and the "bit" or curb, each with its own headstall and reins.

The difference between the bridoon and the ordinary snaffle is one of size; in the former the mouthpiece (always plain) is finer and the rings smaller and rounded.

The bit allows tongue room by a "port" or slight rise in the middle of the mouthpiece. When the bit reins are used, pressure is brought on the bars of the mouth and the

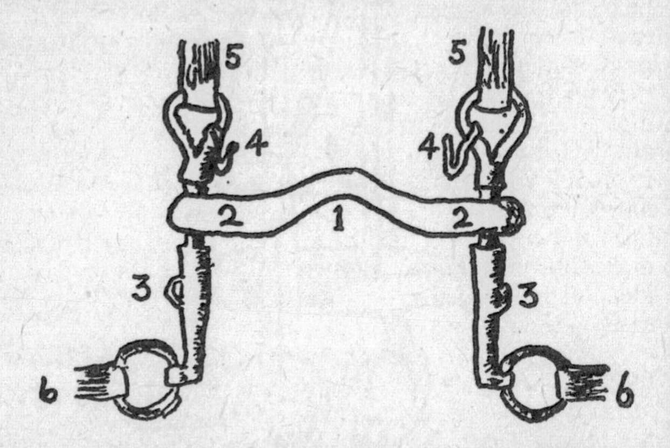

"WEYMOUTH" CURB BIT OF DOUBLE BRIDLE

1. Port
2. Cannons
3. Lip-strap Eyes
4. Curb-chain Hooks
5. Cheek Straps
6. Bit or Curb Reins

port rises—thus it will be seen a high port would bear against the roof of the mouth—and a curb chain presses against the chin groove. The cannons, the straight portions either side of the port, extend slightly outside the mouth, where the cheeks of the bit pass through them, forming a swivel which makes them reversible. The mouthpiece may be twisted on one side, when the smooth surface should lie against the tongue. At the top of the cheeks, small rings are formed to take the headstall and the curb chain hooks. These rings are usually bent slightly outwards, away from the mouth, and this point must be watched for if the bit is reversed. Towards the lower end of each cheek is a small "D" for the lip strap, and at the bottom are the rings for the bit reins.

Double bridles should be adjusted so that the bridoon occupies the position of an ordinary snaffle, the bit lying very slightly below it so that it does not contact the corners of the lips. The curb chain, looped on to the offside hook, is passed *outside* the bridoon and twisted to the right, link by link from that side, so that it lies flat, and is then placed on the nearside hook, again outside the bridoon, at a length which will allow two fingers to be placed edgeways between it and the jaw. It is often advised that the end link should be hooked on first and then the chain shortened to the correct length by following with the appropriate link; in practice it may be found easier to adjust the length first, putting the link on with the thumb uppermost, then looping the last link on top. Curb chains are always far too long, even allowing for the different lengths required, and if you do not have superfluous links removed, neatness can be obtained by hooking up an extra link or two on the offside first to make it even. Do not make the mistake of buying a fine, thin chain with the idea that it is kinder—it is not; a thin chain cuts more easily than a heavy one.

A free "fly-link" will be found running on the centre of the curb chain, and by making your chain even, as recommended, this *will* lie in the centre. Through this fly-link the lip strap is passed and buckled on the near side. One purpose of the lip strap is to prevent the horse taking hold of the cheek of the bit with his lower lip; this would otherwise happen in some cases, but a better reason is to avoid the loss of the chain when unbridling or carrying—chains should, of course, be undone only on the near side when unbridling, but may become detached. Therefore, use a lip strap and keep it buckled when carrying the bridle.

Pelham. The Pelham resembles the bit of the double bridle, and can be regarded as a combination of bit and bridoon. An additional large ring is provided at the mouthpiece on either cheek for the bridoon reins, which are usually referred to as "cheek reins" in this bridle.

In the mouth the Pelham should occupy the position of the curb. In other respects the remarks under "Double Bridle" apply, except that it is common to pass the curb chain through both bridoon rings.

An excellent type of Pelham is that with a slight upward curve in a smooth mouthpiece, in place of the port—the "Mullen-mouth" Pelham (*not* "half-moon"). The advantages of the port are obtained without its disadvantage of possible severity.

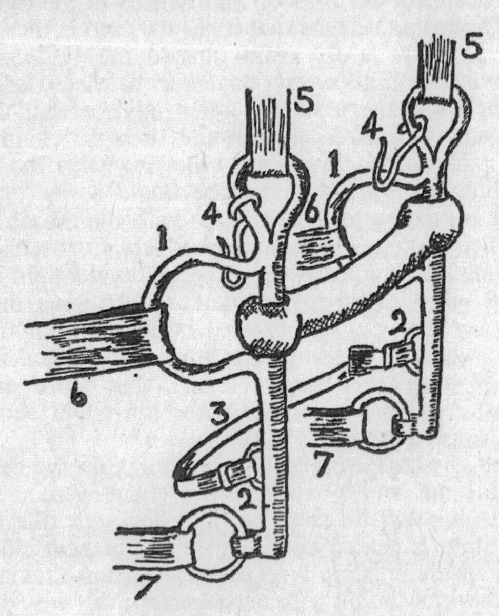

"MULLEN-MOUTH" PELHAM

1. Bridoon (Cheek) Rings
2. Lip-strap Eyes
3. Lip Strap
4. Curb-chain Hooks
5. Cheek Straps
6. Bridoon, Snaffle or Cheek Reins
7. Bit or Curb Reins

Riding Saddles. Saddles are for the comfort of the rider *and the horse*—bareback riding is eventually injurious to the horse's back by bringing weight on the spine instead of on the muscles either side. That being so, the first requirement of any saddle is obvious: even distribution of weight over the back muscles. The distribution of weight must not be extended as far back as the loins, which are a comparatively weak part of the horse's anatomy, nor as far forward as to interfere with the play of the shoulders. Too broad a saddle will bear upon the spine and withers, causing galling, whilst a narrow one will pinch. The principles of saddling have been realised from the earliest times and it is therefore difficult to understand why mistakes are still made. No better example of these principles can be found than the military "Universal" or trooper's saddle, or, nearer civilian standards but still rigidly adhering to correct design, the officer's saddle. These types show, better than any words, how a definite channel must be left over the spine from front to rear, and the uselessness of trying to remedy wither pressure by material placed under the front arch, as is frequently done.

In time the stuffing in the panels becomes flattened and insufficient and permits injurious pressure. If the remedy of restuffing is not immediately possible, a folded blanket may be placed under the saddle but should always be lifted clear of the spine and withers when girthing up, and should always be smooth and unwrinkled and free from any adhering "foreign bodies". Felt pads, called "numnahs", are obtainable for this purpose but need special care since it is difficult to avoid pressure with them. Sheepskin numnahs are excellent and present little trouble in this way, but are rather hot.

Girths. Various materials are used for girths—leather, string, etc., but lampwick (not easily obtained) is possibly the best. The modern nylon ones are strong and easy to wash.

Leather girths are very satisfactory if well cared for but a positive danger when allowed to become hard. A favourite type is the "three-fold", in which there is a wide strip of flannel or similar material which can be soaked with neatsfoot oil to keep the leather supple.

String is probably the best of the cheap materials. It is arranged in rows in the girth and gives secure hold without galling, but particular care must be taken that the strings do not become twisted.

Further information on bridling and saddling will be found in "The Right Way to Ride a Horse".*

* Publisher's Note: by the same author.

SADDLE AND SECTION OF GIRTH

Saddle (Rugby Panel Type)

(A)

1. Pommel
2. Seat
3. Cantle
4. Panel
5. Spring Bar
6. Flap
7. Skirt covering Spring Bar

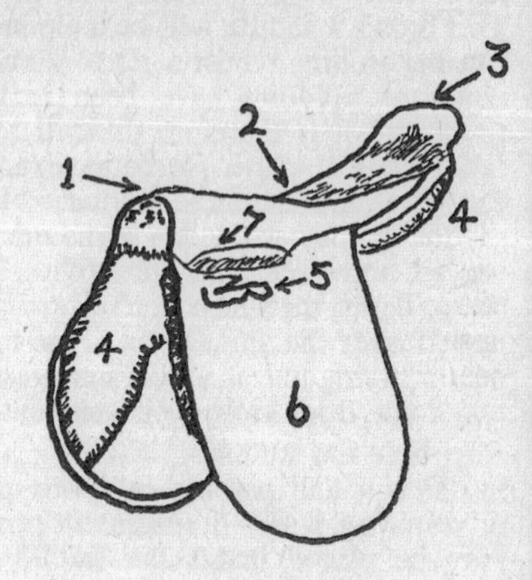

(B)

1. Sweat Flap
2. Girth Leathers or Tabs
3. Portion of Front Arch of Tree

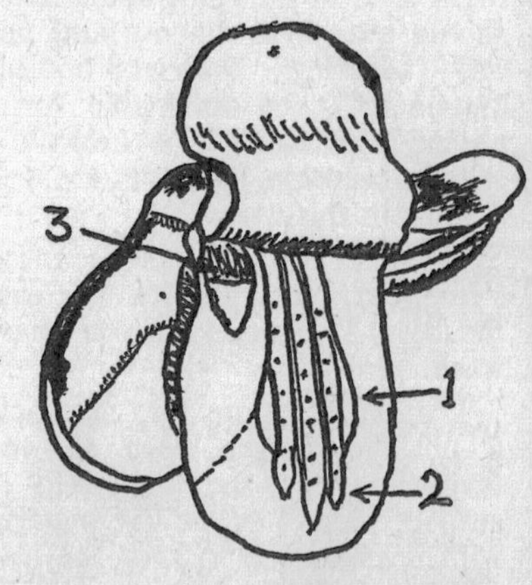

(C)

Fitzwilliam (Webbing) Girth

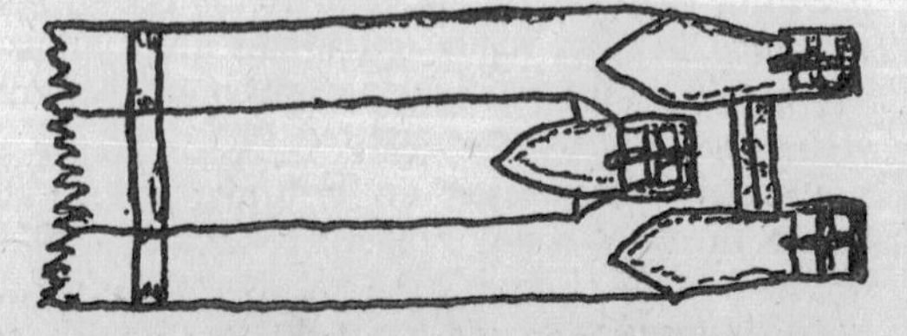

Driving Harness

The parts of driving harness are shown in the diagram on page 121.

Correct Fitting

Collars. The Neck Collar is generally used, and is dealt with here, breast harness being more commonly seen in the old Army transport and artillery. The breast collar, incidentally, is an excellent type, particularly for light work, if the lining is kept scrupulously clean, smooth and supple, and the supporting strap runs over a metal shield on the neck to avoid friction.

Neck collars must fit well and evenly to the shoulders without rubbing, but at the same time they must not be tight and difficult to place, nor must they bear on the neck in front of the withers. It should be possible to insert between the neck and collar: (1) At the top—the flat of the hand. (2) At any part of the sides—the flat of the fingers. (3) At the bottom—the hand and wrist.

Except at the top of the neck, in front of the withers, where galling results from pressure, collar injuries arise from *friction* due to the movement of the shoulder blades. Relief from injuries is best effected by narrower or wider fitting collars, not by the use of pads or chambering (removal of stuffing over an injured part).

The collar is shaped so that it must be turned upside down to pass over the head, then reversed when beyond the ears. Beginners have been noticed trying to put a collar on the wrong way up.

The Hames. The hames are the collar-shaped metal branches in the space between the fore- and afterwale of the collar. If they are not shaped perfectly to the collar, the fit of the latter is upset. They carry the trace bar, and the driving rings for the reins.

Hame or Housing Strap. The purpose of this strap is to bring the sides of the collar together at the top. It must be regularly examined as stretching allows the collar to open slightly, leading to pinching of the neck.

The Saddle or Pad. Like all saddles, this must not bear upon the backbone, and must be kept steady by the girth—

which should not be so tight that a finger cannot be inserted between it and the belly. The bellyband, a continuation of the Back Band supporting the shaft tugs, must have two hands breadth between itself and the belly.

The Crupper. The crupper is connected to the saddle by a Back or Crupper Strap. Its purpose is to prevent forward movement of the saddle and should therefore be no tighter or looser than necessary for this.

Breeching. The breeching should be only slightly above the level of the shafts and hang horizontally. Adjustment is by the Quarter Strap and Loin Strap. Its fitting is important: although it must not allow the saddle to be pushed forward when going downhill or backing, it must not interfere with the movement of the quarters; at other times there should be about four inches between the buttocks and the breeching (when the horse has his weight in the collar).

Traces. These should be hooked in to the trace attachment at a length which keeps the horse clear of the footboard of the vehicle at all times.

Bridle. The remarks under Riding Bridles apply generally. Single bits are used, usually the Liverpool Driving Bit, shown in the diagram, or the double-ringed snaffle which is familiar to everyone. In double harness, that is, for two horses side-by-side, the "Buxton" bit is often seen; this has an additional metal bar between the two cheeks to prevent a rein becoming entangled with the pole. When winkers (or blinkers) are worn, they must allow free vision forward without being loose and flapping, the width being adjusted by the V-strap on the forehead. The avowed object of winkers is to prevent the horse seeing the following wheels, but it would seem we have another example of die-hard custom; winkers were not part of Army draught horse equipment, and nothing was lost in the way of safe driving—or appearance—but, of course, these horses were properly broken to harness work.

Harnessing-up

The collar is put on first, usually with hames and traces attached, the latter loosely knotted out of harm's way. It is turned upside down until the ears are passed, but widening may be necessary first by stretching on the knee or a

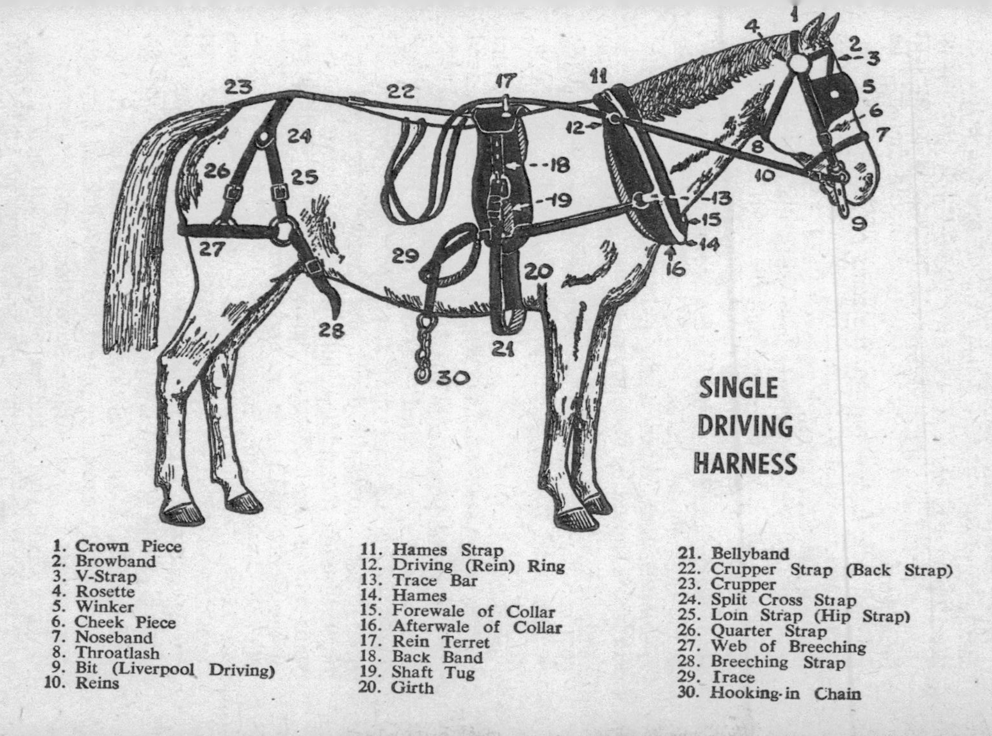
SINGLE DRIVING HARNESS
1. Crown Piece
2. Browband
3. V-Strap
4. Rosette
5. Winker
6. Cheek Piece
7. Noseband
8. Throatlash
9. Bit (Liverpool Driving)
10. Reins
11. Hames Strap
12. Driving (Rein) Ring
13. Trace Bar
14. Hames
15. Forewale of Collar
16. Afterwale of Collar
17. Rein Terret
18. Back Band
19. Shaft Tug
20. Girth
21. Bellyband
22. Crupper Strap (Back Strap)
23. Crupper
24. Split Cross Strap
25. Loin Strap (Hip Strap)
26. Quarter Strap
27. Web of Breeching
28. Breeching Strap
29. Trace
30. Hooking-in Chain

bracket. The Housing Strap must be kept as tight as possible.

Next follow the saddle, crupper and breeching. The saddle is placed slightly *behind* its correct position until the crupper has been passed over the tail into place; it is then adjusted and girthed up, but the bellyband is left unbuckled.

The bridle is now put on, the reins passed through the terrets and fastened to the bit, the spare end being folded through the near terret.

Putting-to. Stand the horse in front of the vehicle, raise the shafts above his back and pull the cart forward; lower and run the shafts through the tugs as far as the stops. Hook in the traces and buckle the breeching around them to the slots on the shafts. Finally, adjust the bellyband.

Unharnessing. When taking a horse out of the shafts, the traces should be undone last as many animals "make a dash" as soon as these are unfastened. The rest of the gear can then be removed in the stable in the normal way, though most people prefer to slip the bridle off before leading in.

Balance of Two-Wheeled Vehicles

To ease the horse, care should be taken to preserve the balance of a two-wheeled vehicle by careful placing of the load—the sliding seat simplifies this. Over-weighting in front forces the shafts down and throws weight on the horse through the saddle, whilst the reverse exerts an upward pull on him. Correctly balanced, there is slight play of the shafts, and gentle up and down movement of the shaft tug buckle at the trot.

Care of Tack

The condition of tack, that is, saddles, bridles, etc., collectively, is a sure guide to the standard of stable-management. A high polish on tack looks very smart, but is unnecessary except in patent leather work on harness; what counts is its condition—cleanliness and suppleness.

When dealing with leather parts, undo all buckles and then wash off grease with *warm* water, dry and vigorously rub in saddle soap. For leather panels and girths, sweat flaps, girth tabs and the *underside* of flaps, there is little better than neatsfoot oil for suppleness and preservation.

On the seat and the outside of flaps, the saddle soap must be well worked in to avoid soiling clothes, but these parts should not be polished. For black harness, special "harness polish" is obtainable. When cleaning girth tabs and stirrup leathers notice should be made of any wear at the holes, and at the parts of the leathers passing through the stirrup irons or over the spring bar. Wear may be reduced by occasionally varying the length of stirrup used, and by raising the girth a hole on one side and lowering on the other. Buckles also should be cleaned and wiped with an oily rag. When buckled bridles are used, do not neglect the leather which takes the wear of the bit rings.

Linen or serge lined saddles and collars should be thoroughly brushed regularly, or it may be necessary to sponge them lightly to remove grease, using the minimum of water. Carefully scraping with a blunt knife, followed by brushing, is a good method of removing grease.

Bits and stirrup irons must be treated according to the material of which they are made. Although plain steel is best, it is not popular with most horsemen because, after washing, it calls for burnishing, rubbing with bath brick, sand and oil, or some similar form of hard labour to produce that appearance possible only in steel. The usual substitutes are stainless steel, nickel or the cheap but unsatisfactory nickel-plating. These only require washing and drying, followed by a rub with a soft cloth; metal polish should not be used on them, but should be reserved for brass fittings. A curb chain polishes well if it is rubbed together between the hands.

18
Mare and foal

THERE is great satisfaction in breeding from one's own mare and rearing and handling the youngster. It is not a difficult branch of horsemastership if, as always, common-sense is used and certain rules are followed. Provided the mare is a suitable type—healthy and "roomy"—the natural process is attended with little trouble.

Stallions are licensed in this country, so defects in that quarter need not be feared; as far as possible, the sire should balance any bad points in the mare, but the best guide is the stock he has been getting. If a stallion cannot be found locally, the Stud Books of the appropriate Breed Society, the Hunter Improvement & National Light Horse Breeding Society, or the National Pony Society, as well as the advertisement columns of "horsey" periodicals, offer plenty of choice.

The Age for Breeding. Fillies and mares are put to the stallion at any age between 2 and 20, but it is safer to avoid extremes, and 4 or 5 years, when they are nearly fully developed, is early enough.

The Month for Breeding. The mare has her oestrus periods normally every three weeks from February until July, lasting up to five days.

In selecting the month for service, we should consider the foal. Obviously the best time for the youngster to make its appearance is when the weather is mild and the grass at its best, so that it has a good start in life; this points to May. Therefore, the average gestation period being 11 months, the ideal time for service is June.

CARE OF THE IN-FOAL MARE

Normally the mare can work to within a month or two of foaling, or later if work is gradually decreased until she is "on half-time". Exercise is necessary to keep her in health, but there must be no strain—avoid heavy pulling and working on deep, holding ground.

The following is a suggested timetable:—

The last two months. The most reliable sign of approaching parturition is swelling of the udder, which is noticeable in the last six to eight weeks. This is more obvious in the morning, and is reduced with exercise. About this time, too, there may in some cases be "waxing", that is the formation of "wax" on the teats; the disappearance of this, giving way to the secretion of milk, usually indicates foaling within twelve hours.

Feeding during the last two months must be generous and of the best. Plenty of good grass will keep her healthy and help in the production of milk; turn the mare out to grass for increasing periods daily, but do this gradually or the digestive system may be upset. Saddle-horses must not be ridden, but should be given walking exercise. Cart mares may do light work in traces; at this time, working in shafts is dangerous for the foal owing to the size of the mare.

The last month. A comfortable, roomy and well-bedded loose-box should be provided for foaling time, and the mare should be sleeping in this now. It is essential that this box should be of ample size to allow free movement and to offer no risk of casting; 12 feet square is the minimum. It should also be well lighted and ventilated and *scrupulously clean.* Before the box is occupied, wash the walls and floor thoroughly, adding disinfectant to the water, then limewash walls and ceiling. The bedding, of the best long straw with the minimum dust and chaff, must be kept clean at all times and soiled portions renewed immediately. A means of observing without disturbing the mare should be arranged in the box, as the less animals are interfered with at these times the better.

Towards the end of the month, feeding must be such as to avoid constipation, and an occasional bran mash is useful. Work should stop a week before foaling.

The owner will find it advisable to have a veterinary inspection of an in-foal mare to decide if parturition is likely to be difficult and to estimate the expected day, so that the practitioner can arrange to be available if necessary.

Foaling day. The more natural the conditions under which the mare has been kept, the less trouble there will be at this time. Foaling is usually straightforward, and fussing must be avoided. The amateur should, however, have an experienced person present, as unless the attendant understands fully what assistance may be required he is likely to do more harm than good. This person should be one familiar to, and trusted by, the mare. Normal "presentation" of the fœtus (about a quarter of an hour after commencement of labour) is with both forefeet first and the head straight and slightly behind them. If about twenty minutes are exceeded in its appearance, it is probable the presentation is abnormal; the skilled assistant, by gently inserting a hand (washed in mild disinfectant and lubricated with olive oil) will be able to detect its nature and possibly adjust a leg or the head carefully into position. Some help in the form of traction may also be required, even in straightforward cases when pain may be reduced in this way.

When the foal is born, it must be seen that it is free of the fœtal membranes and able to breathe. If, even although not so encumbered, the youngster does not begin to breathe, efforts must be made to encourage the action of the lungs by slapping the sides or by pressing at regular intervals on the hinder ribs and the belly. When there is no trouble, the foal will be up and sucking half-an-hour after its delivery.

Although often the umbilical cord breaks naturally during birth or is subsequently bitten through by the mare, as in nature, it is sometimes necessary to cut it with scissors or a knife. In such cases the cord should first be ligatured with tape an inch or two from the belly; two ligatures are often applied, the cut being made between them. The portion at the navel should then be painted with tincture of iodine or dressed with a "safe" disinfectant to guard against the entry of germs. Soiled litter must be removed for burning, and renewed.

The dam should be left alone, if all is well with her, until she has licked the foal, after which she should be given a bran mash with linseed. If she shows no inclination to do this, she may be encouraged by rubbing salt on the foal's coat, otherwise the young animal must be dried with a cloth or some soft hay.

As a final note on this subject, it might be pointed out that, in the usual contrary way of animals, mares often choose the most unexpected time to produce their offspring—not infrequently the one moment when the observer has decided he can be spared.

Care of Mare and Foal

After foaling. Both should stay in the box for a few days, and may then be let out for an hour or two each day in good weather. Food should still be of a laxative nature—plenty of green meal and occasional bran mashes.

Two to three weeks. Both may be sleeping out now, with shelter available. Opportunities should be taken to handle the foal—invaluable lessons for breaking later.

Four weeks. The foal will have learned to nibble grass, and by imitating its mother it learns to eat other food when they are fed together. About this time the mare may be put to light work again, the youngster running with her. Do not let the baby have too much exercise, and allow opportunities for suckling when the mare is not hot or tired. A few weeks before weaning, accustom the new arrival to a foal-slip (small headcollar) during handling; this makes exercise easier afterwards.

Weaning. The usual age for weaning is six months, and the process should be spread over a week. The two should then be kept well apart to enable them to settle down more quickly. The mare's supply of milk will have been decreasing before weaning, but now she must be dried off. By feeding her mainly on the best old hay her milk will quickly disappear, but if it is necessary to draw some off by hand she should not be stripped or the secretion of milk will be encouraged.

The foal will do better with another young companion, and liberal feeding at this stage is important—crushed oats are best, with linseed and small doses of cod liver oil. Continue the daily exercise, which presents more opportunities of handling, and allow an hour or two at grass. Exercise, good feeding and shelter, especially in the first winter, are all-important in giving the animal a good start in life; ground lost now is not easily recovered.

Preparation for breaking. Regular handling from the beginning, as already suggested, greatly simplifies the task of breaking, in fact it forms the first lessons. The voice is of immense value and the foal soon learns to obey simple commands such as "stand", "walk", etc., during leading exercise—"steady" is possibly the most useful word in the horseman's vocabulary, in or out of stables. The dam is an excellent teacher by example while the two are still together. A horse already "broken to voice" will be little trouble in breaking to work. Remember, too, it is essential to have the youngster's confidence; strictly fair, *deserved* correction is quickly understood and appreciated as such whilst the reverse is resented and results in sullenness or bad temper. Particularly is this so in teaching "stable manners". Teach the foal to "move over" and "stand" when told, and accustom it to being stroked all over in preparation for grooming, and to have its feet picked up for grooming and shoeing. The padded pole (see page 61) is useful when this stroking is violently objected to, but gentle persistence is more effective. The owner will now, if ever, realise the importance of selecting a *good* farrier; the feet will have to be trimmed regularly, and for this we need a man who not only knows his job thoroughly but goes about it quietly and with an even temper—and without nervousness. The right farrier is, indeed, a valued assistant in these first breaking lessons.

By gaining the foal's confidence now, future training is made easy and the character of the horse-to-be is formed. Character is more important than conformation.

19
Health and disease

THE objects of this section are to enable the horse keeper, firstly, to eliminate avoidable trouble; secondly, to recognise immediately the first signs of ill-health so that treatment may be applied in the early stages, when it is most effective; thirdly, to co-operate with his veterinarian either by intelligent assistance or, at least, by not increasing his difficulties. No suggestion is made that treatment of any but the least serious complaints and injuries should be attempted by the layman. It is foolish for an amateur to interfere on the strength of only vague knowledge of veterinary matters, or to experiment with patent "cure-alls" of the composition and effects of which he is ignorant. The only humane and economic way is to obtain the services of an expert, qualified man. He can, however, ease the professional's task by supplying all relevant information, by anticipation of provisions likely to be necessary, and by carrying out instructions faithfully and intelligently. The Veterinary Surgeon, unlike the doctor, is handicapped from the beginning in that he must discover for himself such facts as will enable him accurately to diagnose, without verbal assistance from his patient.

First Signs of Trouble. Ill-health can be recognised by any departure from the normal spirits, appearance and behaviour.

Unless any of the following are normal in the particular animal, they should be regarded with suspicion:—Unusual attitude or stance; dullness and a tendency to mope and avoid companions; changed appetite; "tight" skin or harsh "staring" coat; unusual breathing; marked uneasiness; excessive sweating; abnormality in the droppings. These are only general indications. To diagnose the particular trouble they must be linked up with specific symptoms or known conditions.

When any of these signs are noticed, examine the horse carefully. It may be a trivial matter which you can put

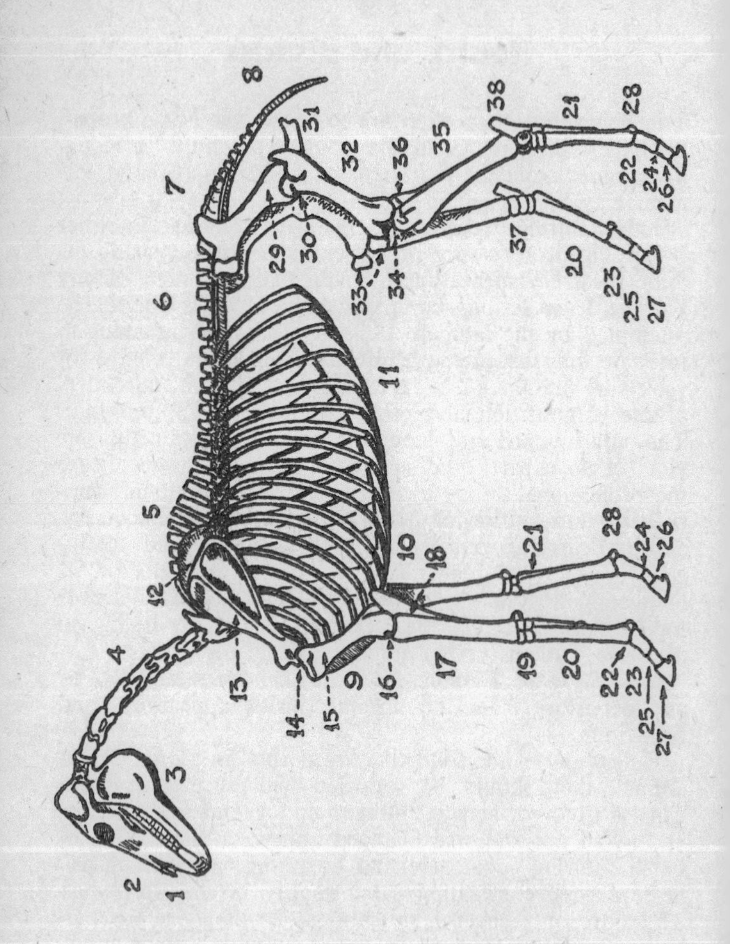
1
2
3
4
5
6
7
8
9
10
11
12
13
14
15
16
17
18
19
20
21
22
23
24
25
26
27
28
22
23
24
25
26
27
28
20
21
29
30
31
32
33
34
35
36
37
38

SKELETON

Axial (Head, Neck and Trunk)

1. Nasal Bone
2. Upper Jaw
3. Lower Jaw
4. 7 Cervical (Neck) Vertebræ
5. 18 Dorsal (Back) Vertebræ
6. 6 Lumbar (Loin) Vertebræ
7. 5 Sacral Vertebræ forming Sacrum (Croup)
8. 17 Caudal (Tail) Vertebræ
9. Sternum (Breastbone)
10. 8 pairs True Ribs (on Breastbone)
11. 10 pairs False Ribs
12. Cartilage of prolongation

Appendicular (Limbs)

13. Scapula (Shoulder Blade)
14. Shoulder Joint
15. Humerus (Upper Arm Bone)
16. Elbow Joint
17. Radius (Forearm)
18. Ulna (Human "funny bone")
19. Carpus (Knee)
20. Cannon Bone
21. Splint Bone
22. Fetlock Joint
23. Os Suffraginis (Long Pastern)
24. Pastern Joint
25. Os Corona (Coronet Bone—Short Pastern)
26. Coffin Joint
27. Os Pedis (Coffin or Pedal Bone)
28. Sesamoid Bones
29. Ilium (Haunch)
30. Hip Joint
31. Ischium (Point of Buttock)
32. Femur (Upper Thigh Bone)
33. Patella (Knee Cap)
34. Stifle Joint
35. Tibia (Large Lower Thigh Bone)
36. Fibula (Small Lower Thigh Bone)
37. Tarsus (Hock Joint)
38. Os Calcis (Heel Bone—Point of Hock)

right yourself. If the horse is lying down, do not immediately rush to the 'phone, he may only be resting. The Veterinary Surgeon is a busy man, and it is unfair to him and other people in charge of animals to call him out unnecessarily; attention to a more serious case may be delayed through his absence.

If you decide attention is necessary, note everything you can about the case that may be of assistance to the Veterinary Surgeon in forming his opinion as to its urgency, the treatment likely to be necessary and any instruments that may be required. With this information he may also be able to give advice over the telephone for emergency treatment until his arrival.

When he arrives, be ready for him and give him all the known *facts,* even apparently trivial ones may be useful, but remember he will not be interested in your theories.

For his inspection he may require your help in various ways.

To Get a Horse Up. It is usually ineffective to try to coax a horse up. Put on his headcollar (this gives you more control than a halter). and with a jerk on the rope call him sharply. Be sure there is plenty of litter under his feet, to avoid slipping, stand well away and give him room so that he does not hit himself or you when scrambling to his feet.

Holding for Examination. This is done in a similar way to leading in or out of the stable: Stand in front of the horse and facing him, with a hand either side of the headcollar or bridle. While the hindquarters are being examined, it is often advisable, to prevent kicking, to hold up a forefoot. Run your hand down the back tendons to the fetlock joint, press, and speak to the horse, then just let the toe of the foot rest on your fingers when he has lifted it.

"Trotting-up." You may be asked to "run him up", that is, trot him directly away and then back to the examiner. If the animal is quiet, this may be done in a halter or headcollar, but a snaffle bridle is better for control and the reins should be taken over the head. Walk or run on the near side, with the reins slack and held about a foot or eighteen inches from the bit, leaving the head free. Look where you are going, not at the horse, and if you have difficulty in making him trot do not pull at him, he must be driven forward by an assistant. When turning,

unless you have been told otherwise, stop and turn to the right so that you do not obscure the examiner's view. Usually turns have to be made sharply, with the hindlegs as a pivot.

General Symptoms

These serve as a guide in diagnosis, and any one of them in conjunction with one or more others, may indicate the ailment. Similarly, the absence of a symptom is useful in eliminating the possibility of a particular complaint.

Temperature. The normal temperature varies between approximately 100 and 101 degrees Fahrenheit. It is taken by inserting the thermometer in the rectum for at least three minutes. When it has to be taken over a period, the same time each day should be chosen as there are variations during the course of the day; the temperature is normally higher at midday and in the evening that at other times. A temperature that rises during the night is regarded as dangerous.

Infectious diseases are always accompanied by a rise in temperature, which is often the first symptom. It is a wise precaution, therefore, to separate an animal "with a temperature" from others, and to take steps to avoid carrying the infection or contagion to healthy animals. An infectious disease is one which can be spread indirectly, usually by the breath, whilst contagion is spread by contact, directly or indirectly. Both are frequently used loosely and considered interchangeable, and many diseases are both infectious and contagious.

For general treatment of fever, the instructions under "Food and Water" on page 136 should be followed, and in the early stages a mild laxative is of value—a dose of from ½ to 3 ozs. of Glauber or Epsom Salts, according to age and size, in the food or water, is recommended.

Pulse. It is not easy to detect changes in the pulse, but it can be felt with the first two fingers where the submaxillary artery crosses the lower jaw, at the inside of the elbow or immediately above the fetlock. The rate is normally about 35 to 40 per minute, being faster in feverish conditions, and slower in debility.

Appetite. Generally, the horse is a greedy feeder, always ready for a meal, and a poor appetite is suspicious. Distinction must be made between loss of appetite and inability or difficulty in eating; most horses will make valiant attempts to eat, even with obstruction or injury in the mouth or throat.

Refusing food may be due to overwork, when a rest, a gruel or a mash will be followed by a return of the appetite.

Difficulty in eating, and "quidding"—allowing food to drop out of the mouth after an attempt to chew—may indicate trouble with the teeth, injury or obstruction in the mouth or throat, or soreness.

An abnormal or depraved appetite is frequently noticed when worms are present, or in indigestion. It may be due to "vice", such as crib-biting—gnawing woodwork, etc.

Refusing to drink is often simply due to some objection to the water or container—dirt or odour.

Attitude. Normally the horse stands with the forefeet planted firmly and squarely, but frequently rests a hind-foot.

Resting or "pointing" a forefoot, that is, placing it in advance of the other when standing, usually on the toe, is to relieve it of weight and indicates trouble in that foot, possibly laminitis—inflammation of the sensitive structures. If there is trouble in the two forefeet, both are placed forward. When the forelegs are held wide apart it is usually a sign of chest affection. Continual pawing and scraping with the toe may be because of disease of the navicular bone, or the manifestation of pain.

If the hindfeet are drawn well forward and there is reluctance to back, suspect trouble in those feet.

Inability to rise follows tetanus (lockjaw), sprained back muscles, spinal injury, etc.

General uneasiness, constantly lying down and getting up again, is often the result of stomach pains (colic, for example) and when these are severe, the symptom is accompanied by quick, laboured breathing.

Constant stamping, or rubbing one leg against the other, is often caused by the invasion of mites giving rise to irritation. The condition is sometimes called "itchy heels" and is more often found in heavy draught horses with much feathering on the legs.

An unusual amount of scratching, biting, and rubbing against trees or other convenient hard objects, should lead to an inspection for insects, such as lice.

Breathing. The respirations may be judged by watching or feeling the rise and fall of the flanks, and by the expiration of breath from the nostrils. When at rest, the breathing should be noiseless, steady and even, the normal respirations being about 10–15 per minute.

Breathing sounds usually point to affections of the nose, throat or lungs.

Quickened breathing is present in most chest complaints and when in conjunction with general uneasiness is a sign of great pain, as in severe colic.

Painful breathing may be looked for in pleurisy.

Doubled expirations, that is, with two separate efforts, especially when audible, often mean that the wind is affected.

Excreta. The droppings should be passed in small balls which break on the ground, golden brown in stable-fed, greenish in grass-fed horses.

If they are too hard or soft, digestive disturbance is to be suspected.

From an inspection of the dung, worms or their eggs may be detected.

The urine is rather thick and yellow in health, but has a bright colour when there is fever.

Membranes. The visible membranes, the linings of the eyes, nose and mouth, should be pink and moist. There is a yellowish tinge in liver complaints; paleness in anæmia; reddening and dryness in fever, and purple spotting with impurity of the blood.

Skin and Coat. The skin should be supple and elastic, and the coat should lie flat and smooth, with a certain amount of gloss.

When any of these qualities are missing it is usually because the digestion is out of order. The coat will, of course, "stare" or stand up, when the animal is cold, but apart from this may be a warning of worms. A scurfy coat, if not through lack of grooming, may be caused by a skin disease such as mange. Mange, incidentally, is a notifiable disease, as your Vet. will tell you.

Excessive sweating, unless due to weather conditions or hard work, often results from general weakness but is sometimes a symptom of great pain or tetanus.

20
Nursing of sick horses

THE general management of sick animals is an important part of their treatment and has great effect on speed of recovery and subsequent restoration to full strength and fitness.

Stabling and Exercise. In favourable weather the paddock makes the best sick-bay for most cases. A run at grass provides three essentials, unlimited fresh air, sunlight and natural food, together with gentle exercise which the animal can regulate to his own requirements.

When weather conditions or the particular ailment make stabling necessary, ample ventilation without draughts must be assured. Bedding should be plentiful and fulfil all requirements, being dry, clean, elastic and level, to encourage proper rest. Quiet is essential in all cases, but particularly in nervous diseases, when it may be advisable to darken the windows. In serious illness it should be the rule that no one but the person in charge of the patient is allowed in or near the box, whether or not there is risk of carrying infection; this will eliminate at least some unnecessary disturbance and noise.

The need for meticulous cleanliness of stable, feeding and drinking bowls, cannot be over-emphasised. If possible a special "sick box" should be reserved, and this should have the walls lime-washed, preferably blue which is found to be disliked by flies. A good disinfectant, such as Jeyes, should be at hand in every stable at all times, and will be an asset during sickness; the air in the stable may also be sprayed with it in the event of infectious diseases.

Food and Water. It is in dealing with sickness that a horse keeper's claim to be a "good feeder" is most severely tested.

Whilst the corn ration should be reduced according to the duration of illness, every effort must be made to keep up condition. The best hay obtainable will form most of the diet and it will usually be of value to include some bran, but the value of green fodder and roots must not be overlooked. It is very necessary to keep the bowels in good order, and fresh green food is ideally suited for this as well as being acceptable to the poorest appetite which needs tempting. Linseed and bran mashes, gruel, etc., will be found useful.

Certain principles must be observed: small quantities of the most easily digested food are to be given at frequent, regular intervals. No uneaten food is to be left in the stable in the hope that the horse may eat it in time—he will not; since it becomes tainted with his own saliva and with unavoidable odours, he will soon lose any appetite he had. Feeding cannot be forced. A poor appetite may be tempted by offering variety, particularly in debility, and the addition of salt is often a means of making food more attractive and of encouraging the appetite. When there is disturbance of the digestive system, good results may follow from withholding food for several hours—this might be recommended also for humans.

Clean water should always be available, but it must be renewed frequently as, like other food, it soon becomes tainted. In cold weather it may, with advantage, have the chill taken off.

Clothing and Bandages. The temperature must be regulated to avoid extremes, and the best way of maintaining body warmth without denying fresh air is by clothing, which can be reduced or increased as circumstances demand. Over-clothing must be avoided; to a weak animal heavy rugs can be tiring and may further weaken him by causing sweating. Carefully observe all the rules of rugging-up: comfortable fitting, no interference with movement or breathing, and no chafing. In summer, light linen "summer sheets" will be found an advantage as protection from flies.

Bandages may be necessary for warmth or other purposes, and, again, the rules must be strictly followed: no tightness to interfere with the circulation or with movement, and they must be rolled on evenly. They should be removed at intervals during the day, and the limbs rubbed to improve circulation before replacing. Woollen bandages are best, and if less elastic material is used, a layer of cotton wool should be placed underneath, with special attention to joints and swollen parts. Wounds are bandaged as little as possible, since, if kept clean, air and sun are valuable healing agents. This is a point the Veterinary Surgeon will decide, and he will probably make himself solely responsible for the actual bandaging, at least in serious cases. If you have to bandage a wound, do so in such a manner that will bring any hanging piece of skin back into position and do not bind tightly on the wound itself. Except with profuse bleeding, all you need is covering and protection.

For reducing swelling from sprain, cold water bandages are not very effective; they almost immediately lose their first chill and soon assume body heat, necessitating constant renewal. Similarly, hot water bandages for the same purpose, soon reduce to body temperature and become ineffective. In the majority of cases, hosing with cold water for a quarter of an hour two or three times a day answers best.

Grooming. Cleanliness of the skin and coat is more necessary during sickness than at any other time. Grooming, besides achieving this, gives a better feeling of well-being and comfort and should not be omitted unless the nature of the case makes it impossible or undesirable. Remember to attend to the feet also. Perform these duties quickly, quietly and efficiently; this is no time for fussing and irritating the horse.

Administering Medicine. I have always stressed the similarity between horses and children, and never is this more noticeable than when medicines have to be given. "Gentleness and guile" is the motto when trying to get medicines into the right place.

Powders, thoroughly mixed with the favourite food, are usually taken without any trouble, but horses have an acute sense of smell and easily detect any tampering with their food, so include some choice ingredient such as grated carrots well mixed in—or whatever is the particular fancy of your animal. A sprinkling of the same delicacy on top always proves tempting and lulls suspicion.

Liquid medicines, or "drenches", are best given from a long-necked bottle or a "drenching horn". Raise the horse's head as high as possible, or horizontal, and let the drench trickle in *small* quantities on the *back* of the tongue. Keep the head raised until you are certain he has swallowed—you will know when, if you have ever watched a horse drinking and seen the swallowing movements at the lower side of the neck. Patience will be called for, as most horses will hold liquid medicines for a long time, to be returned to the unwary when their heads are free. There is no guile in drenching, but gentleness is all-important to avoid active resistance and, possibly, broken glass.

21
Ailments of the leg and foot

Lameness

Seats of Lameness. The parts in which lameness most commonly occurs are *below the knee or hock, particularly the foot and the back tendons.* The knee itself, a complicated joint with many small bones which distribute and minimise concussion, suffers least. The shoulder, too, is comparatively seldom affected, and when it is, the muscles are usually the seat of injury by sprains or blows. Below the knee and hock there are no muscles, and the tendons normally bear the strain—if they do not the bone will fracture.

When the position of lameness cannot be immediately located, the usual practice is to suspect the foot; the old saying advises us to "remove the shoe, even if the horse is lame in the head", and so many troubles originate in the foot that this is sound advice. Here diagnosis is difficult, since the mechanism is completely hidden in the horny box of the hoof.

Which Leg? The question has caused a very great deal of head-scratching and dispute, and many a sound leg has been long and religiously treated by mistake. The following points are a guide to solving the problem.

As indicated in "Signs of Health", standing in the stable the horse may "point", or rest, a lame foreleg in front of the other, while resting a hindleg is normal. Constant uneasiness on one foot is also suspicious.

If such signs are absent, the horse should be taken out on to a smooth hard surface and "trotted up"—slowly away from and then back to the examiner. It may be possible to gain a clue from any "favouring" of the affected limb and "dropping", or bearing more heavily, on the sound one. He should be trotted up directly he is brought out of the stable, preferably after a rest, when stiffness is more pronounced.

Nodding the head at the trot is a reliable indication. When lame in front, it is dipped as the sound leg touches the ground, and raised on the lame one. Severe lameness in both forelegs often gives the impression of soundness, but, watching the action, "pottering" or stepping short, is noticeable. While determining the leg, in this way, it is often possible to find the position of the trouble. Turning the leg outwards indicates the knee or elbow, while dragging the toe, due to difficulty in forward movement of the leg, means the shoulder.

In a hindleg, lameness is shown when trotting away by the hock of the sound one rising higher and dipping lower than the other. When trotting back, the head nods on the injured leg. The first, however, is not an infallible sign; it may be due to spinal injury.

Finding the Position. The affected leg found, it should be felt for heat, tenderness or enlargements, and carefully compared with the sound one. If it appears normal, the next step is to have the shoe taken off and the foot searched for nails, bruises, corns, etc. "Pointing" usually means the trouble is in the foot, as does constantly lifting the foot—the latter indicating great pain.

Causes of Lameness. Horses doing fast work on soft ground frequently suffer from strain of the tendons and ligaments, encouraged by bad riding, working when tired or on unsuitable "going".

Following long work on hard surfaces, particularly in draught horses, bony enlargements may appear, and it is while these are forming that lameness occurs. Neglected enlargements soon spread and sometimes interfere with the movement of joints. A stilted action and sprain of the "check ligament", showing as a painful swelling immediately below the knee, are also liable to result from such work. The check ligament is the one which enables a horse to sleep standing, and is situated with the back tendons between the knee and fetlock.

Dislocations. When a joint is dislocated, the ligaments and muscles connected with it are usually sprained at the same time. Dislocations are known as "congenital" (during the period of gestation), "acquired" or "accidental", and "pathological" (from disease).

Partial dislocations are commonly met with in young animals, at the fetlock or the patella (the "knee cap" in the stifle joint), when restoration is simple—in fact the bone can often be heard to click back into position of its own accord. Complete dislocation is more serious, but where muscles are more concerned than ligaments in holding the joint together, as in the shoulder, there is greater hope of full recovery.

The symptoms of dislocation are deformity, loss of use of the limb together with a shortening of it, and often painful swelling.

Smaller bones may be replaced by extension and counter extension, under an anæsthetic. Others may be restored by manipulation also, with the application of a biniodide blister—a counter-irritant ointment—which will assist in strengthening strained ligaments.

Immediate skilled attention is necessary for all cases.

Fractures. Fractures may be partial or complete, and are known as simple, compound, comminuted, impacted, or greenstick.

Simple fractures are unaccompanied by external wounds, and the split may be across the bone (transverse), at an angle (oblique) or the full length of the bone (longitudinal).

Compound fractures show an external wound.

Comminuted fractures may be simple or compound, and the term means that the bone is broken into more than two portions—as in crushing.

Impacted fractures are those where the broken parts have been driven into each other.

Greenstick fractures are incomplete splits, much in the manner that a green stick breaks. This kind is more common in young stock, whose bones are not so brittle as adults'.

Symptoms generally are pain and loss of function, followed by swelling. There is not the "fixing" of the parts which appears in a dislocation, and the broken parts can be heard grating on each other—"crepitation".

Treatment must wait until any swelling has been reduced by warm fomentations. If there is no swelling, or it has subsided, extension and counter-extension may restore the broken parts, followed by splints to keep them in place. A thick layer of cotton wool should be wrapped round the limb first, then splints of any convenient material applied reaching from the joint below to the one above, the whole bandaged in position. Care must be taken that splinters of bone are not forced into the skin in the process. The wound of a compound fracture must be left unbandaged or part of the bandage cut away over it, and must be given appropriate cleansing treatment. Bandages must not be tight enough to interfere with the circulation, and massage will be necessary after their removal. Serious fractures usually have to result in the death of the animal, owing to expense and difficulty in treatment. It is better for the amateur not to interfere, in most cases; the best he can do is to fix the limb with splints, without attempting reduction, while waiting for the Veterinary Surgeon.

See also the appropriate sections: "Forelegs" and "Hindlegs".

Rheumatism. Rheumatism frequently gives rise to lameness, and may be due to bad stabling conditions, and the symptom is usually stiffness. Local treatment with embrocation, vigorously rubbed in, helps when the affected part is located, but Rheumatism (as most human sufferers know!) has a knack of "dodging about" from one place to another in a bewildering manner. Advice on internal treatment should be obtained—bad cases respond to salicylate of soda, or a deficiency of phosphorus may have to be made good—but stabling should receive attention.

Sprains. The bones comprising joints are held together by ligaments, strong bands of tissue which protect them from over-extension. Muscles are attached to bones upon which they act, by tendons ("sinews" or "leaders"), almost inelastic cords which permit the full elasticity of muscles being used without injury.

When subjected to injury or excessive strain, from blows, sudden twists, concussion, etc., sprain of the ligaments or tendons results, accompanied by swelling, stiffness and tenderness. Sprains are a common cause of lameness in the horse, and treatment is simple but neglect may lead to permanent stiffness of the joint. It sometimes happens that the bones themselves are injured or fractured, and it is always wise to have professional assistance when the sprain is severe.

In all cases, immediate rest is essential. A week or a fortnight may be sufficient for mild sprains, but it is no use being in a hurry to resume work. Horses that have suffered from bad sprains benefit from a run at grass for a month or two after recovery. In the early stages, inflammation can be reduced by cold water; when possible, turning a hose on the affected part for a quarter of an hour three or four times a day is recommended. Failing this, either cold or hot water bandages may be applied, and should be renewed frequently otherwise they soon become ineffective. For less simple cases, an antiphlogistine dressing is good; the proprietary "antiphlogistine" is applied hot on a layer of cotton wool held firmly in place by a bandage of elastic material. Support may later be useful, and should consist of a thick wrapping of cotton wool under a stout bandage of stuff like calico; pressure aggravates the trouble, so they should be removed daily and the limbs massaged before re-bandaging. Blisters, usually mercurial ointments, are also often employed to strengthen the ligaments, but their use should be on the advice of a Veterinary Surgeon. One of the well-known horse embrocations may be helpful; they are, in fact, a mild form of blister, but possibly much of their value lies in the massage entailed.

Foot Trouble

In a healthy foot the wall is cool and sound, the sole hard but not brittle, and there is no offensive smell when normally clean.

The following are the commonest foot complaints and injuries, with notes on symptoms and treatment. Do not hesitate to seek professional advice when they are discovered.

Brittle Hoof. This is often a natural defect and is seen mostly in hot, dry weather. It makes shoeing difficult, as the hoof breaks away and gives little nail-hold, often leading to nails being driven too close to the sensitive structures and causing lameness. The application of oils to the crust (Neatsfoot Oil or Hoof Oil) increases the pliancy of the horn, whilst embrocation to the coronet, every other day, helps to promote growth.

Canker. This is a diseased condition of the sole, in which a greyish fungus forms, and is caused by injuries or neglect of elementary cleanliness of the foot. Lameness seldom results. Amateur treatment is not advised, but the foot must be kept dry, particular attention paid to the bedding, and antiseptic dressings, such as powdered alum, applied.

Corns. These are bruises of the sensitive sole, at the angle of the heels, and may lead to abscesses. Concussion and pressure of the heel of the shoe, from faulty shoeing, are common causes, and flat and weak feet are most liable. The "economical" practice of keeping shoes on too long, so that the wall overlaps them, is a fruitful source of corns. The horse must be rested, without shoes; damaged horn should be removed and a cold bran poultice applied. When work is resumed it is advisable to use special shoes that relieve the sole of pressure.

Cracked Heels. This is an inflamed condition of the heels, in which fluid collects under the skin, and which causes acute lameness for a few steps until the skin cracks and releases a greasy discharge, giving immediate relief. Lameness recurs when, after resting, the skin heals and fluid again forms. The most common cause is wetting the heels when washing the legs, and not drying properly, but there is sometimes constitutional predisposition. The wound should be cleansed, dried and dusted with boric powder, or oxide of zinc ointment used. Daily exercise is necessary to prevent trapping of fluid under the skin, and precautions must be taken against future trouble.

Cracks in the Wall. Cracks may start from the ground surface, in which case they are not usually serious and will grow out, or they may begin from the Coronet. The latter, known as "Sandcracks", need careful attention. The condition arises for many reasons—removal of the Periople during shoeing, fast work on hard ground, injury, and sometimes badly-formed limbs. There are several ways of dealing with them, but the cracks should be cleaned out and pressure relieved by cutting away the wall at the part of the ground surface in line with them. Following this they may be gradually closed by clipping together or by a strap or tarred string around the hoof, and with special shoeing.

False Quarter. This is a defect in which a thin layer of brittle horn forms on the wall, and occurs mostly at the sides, where it is seen as a groove or series of grooves rather like Sandcracks. There is no lameness, but weakness of the foot. Since it arises from the Coronary Band—

after injury, Quittor (page 147), etc.—a blister to the Coronet is the usual treatment. If the horn has cracked badly, it should be eased from pressure on the shoe by cutting out a nick in the wall at the point of bearing, as in Sandcrack. Special shoeing may be advisable.

Forging. The common term for this, "Clicking", gives the clue to the trouble, striking a fore-shoe with a hind, usually at the trot. It seldom causes injury, although it may obviously be dangerous in some circumstances, but the continual click is annoying. Unschooled and unbalanced horses, and those out of condition, are generally the culprits. A concave shoe may help in curing the noise. See "Shoeing".

Founder, or Laminitis. This is an inflammation of the foot, usually a forefoot, shown by reluctance to move and standing with the greater part of the weight on the hind-legs. The inflammation may be brought on by over-feeding. The animal should have his shoes removed and be put in a loose-box where he can be moved around. Cold bran poultices should be applied to the foot and kept wet.

Grogginess (Navicular Disease). Navicular Disease or ulceration of the Navicular Bone is, among other reasons, sometimes due to hereditary causes or the inability of the frog to absorb concussion. The symptoms are "pointing" and a short-stepping action, moving on the toes, which makes the trouble more obvious when travelling downhill and wears the shoes rapidly at this part. Complete cure can never be guaranteed, but with care the horse may resume work. Cold water to reduce inflammation, and later special shoeing, are the usual form of treatment. Regular exercise, or at least the use of a loose-box when the animal must stand in for some time, is a means of prevention.

Over-Reach. The upper part of the forefoot, at the heels or higher, is often cut by the toe of the hind at the gallop; an uncollected horse is always liable to over-reach, or it may be caused by weakness, when jumping, or pulling up sharply. The injury requires wound treatment, washing with cold water and dressing antiseptically, and endeavours must be made to prevent its recurrence—see "Shoeing".

Pricks. There are two ways in which a foot may be pricked: (1) in shoeing, (2) by picking up a nail or similar object. The first will usually be evident at the time and is the farrier's responsibility. In either case, the shoe must be removed as soon as possible and the foot poulticed every four hours with bran and hot water with a tablespoonful of disinfectant, to draw out any poison. This treatment, of course, is not always possible if the injury takes place out of doors. In such a case, the sharp object must be withdrawn at once and hot water poured on the wound. Alternatively, the wound should be cauterized by heating and running the same nail, piece of wire, etc., into the hole again with the minimum of delay, afterwards pressing in ordinary soap. On return to stables, have the shoe removed and the foot properly treated.

Quittor. This is a fistulous sore in the Coronet, often resulting from a prick in which the pus has been allowed to work its way upwards and through the Coronary Band. The sore should be antiseptically washed and, if present, the wound in the sole opened and poulticed.

Sandcrack. See "Cracks in the Wall".

Seedy Toe. In Seedy Toe, the white line is injured by inflammation, affecting the secretion of horn and causing separation between the hoof casing and the horny laminæ, starting at the toe. Laminitis is generally to blame, but it occasionally arises from weakness or from pressure by the shoe clip. It is noticeable, when the shoe is removed, by the absence of the white line in places, or the hollowness can be detected by tapping the wall. The cavity exposed on removal of the shoe must be probed and cleaned; part of the wall may have to be rasped away to remove mealy horn, and it should be kept wet with cold swabs. A soft, thick bed, such as peat moss, is recommended in view of the soreness of the foot. In shoeing, pressure should be avoided.

Sidebones. This is ossification of one or more Lateral Cartilages, generally caused by concussion or strain, often with hereditary predisposition. Heavy cart horses are most likely to suffer. The Lateral Cartilages are found at the back of the wall and surround the Plantar Cushion. Ossification is shown by bulging of the wall and, perhaps, very uneven wear in the shoe. In the early stages, hot fomentation and rubbing in embrocation may arrest the trouble. Pathological shoeing is necessary.

Thrush. Thrush is the term employed when the frog is diseased and has an offensive discharge from the cleft—

this discharge has a characteristic, cheesy smell that cannot be mistaken. It does not generally lame, but the horn decomposes and canker may follow. The commonest reason is neglect, and continual standing in wet, filthy bedding, but bad shoeing, paring the frog or otherwise denying normal pressure, is also a cause. Cleanliness and correct functioning of the frog are the first essentials in its prevention and cure. First the foot must be cleaned thoroughly, by washing with antiseptics. Afterwards it must be kept dry and dressed with one of the following: Bluestone; Stockholm Tar plugged in on a piece of tow; boracic acid; calomel powder; or even common salt if nothing else is available.

Treads. These are similar wounds to Over-Reaches but are inflicted on the hindfeet by the front toe of another horse. Because of the danger of this, riders should always keep a full horse-length behind the animal in front when going in single file. Treatment is the same as for Over-Reaches.

The Pastern and Fetlock

Brushing. This defective action, in either the fore or hindlegs, is striking or brushing the lower part of one leg—usually at the fetlock or the coronet—with the opposite foot. Although at most times trifling, it may cause swelling of the part and lameness. Bad conformation, tiredness, poor condition and faulty shoeing are all causes. When due to the first, the only prevention is the use of a "Brushing" or "Yorkshire Boot", of felt or rubber, fitting over the fetlock joint, or an exercise bandage as a substitute. See also "Speedy Cutting".

Dislocations. Young animals are subject to partial dislocation of the fetlock, which may easily be replaced. In adult working horses, the fetlock of a foreleg has less hope of complete recovery, but partial displacement of a hind fetlock often gives little trouble. See page 141.

Fractures. See page 142.

Ringbone. Ringbone is a bony enlargement on either or both the long and short pasterns, and is termed "high" or "low" according to position. The chief danger is interference with the pastern joint. The condition develops as the result of a direct blow or concussion, but there is often hereditary predisposition. When forming, Ringbone produces a "pottering" lameness, but the enlargement is difficult to detect at this stage, especially when so low that it is situated under the Coronet, where it may not be noticed until the wall bulges. In any case of unaccountable lameness it is wise to suspect Ringbone—in fact it could be said that the "symptom" of a developing Ringbone is the *absence* of symptoms (except lameness). Treatment is tedious and prolonged, cure difficult and uncertain. There is reasonable hope of the animal being later fit for slow work, however, if treatment begins immediately lameness is noticed. Rest at once, without shoes, either in a well-littered loose-box or turned out on soft ground, to allow expansion of the hoof to relieve the bones. Cold applications and blistering will help, and pathological shoeing should be considered later.

Sesamoiditis. The term means, of course, inflammation of the small Sesamoid Bones situated behind the fetlock. It arises from injury either to the bones or their ligaments or tendons, setting up inflammation. There is swelling and tenderness of the joint, which appears to be displaced forwards, and the lameness causes short-stepping. In the early stages the inflammation can be reduced by rest and cold water. Support should be given by a loose, thick layer of cotton wool securely held by a bandage of some firm material such as calico; the trouble must not be aggravated by pressure, and the bandage should be removed and renewed daily. Counter-irritants may be required later.

Sprains. In this region, sprains are occasionally confused with Ringbone, but since the sinews are near the surface it is possible to differentiate by feel. See also page 143.

THE FORELEG: BELOW THE KNEE

Back Tendons. Most saddle horses are liable to sprain of these tendons from an unlucky twist or from concussion when jumping. Frequent resting of the leg and stepping short are the first signs, followed by swelling. After sprain treatment (page 143) a long rest at grass is advised.

Breakdown. This term includes any fractures or sprains which permit the fetlock to drop, sometimes as far as the ground. It occurs most commonly in horses of speed and spells finish to their career on the course or in the hunting field. When only slight, eventual recovery may take place, but only slow work will be possible. Long, professional treatment is required, and while waiting for attention the hollow of the heel should be packed with any soft material at hand, bandaged in position. Cold water will help to reduce inflammation, and after recovery there should be a long rest at grass.

Speedy Cutting. This is similar to Brushing, but the injury is inflicted higher on the leg, often on the inside of the knee. Cause and treatment are as for Brushing.

Splint. A bony exostosis, or extra growth, joining the

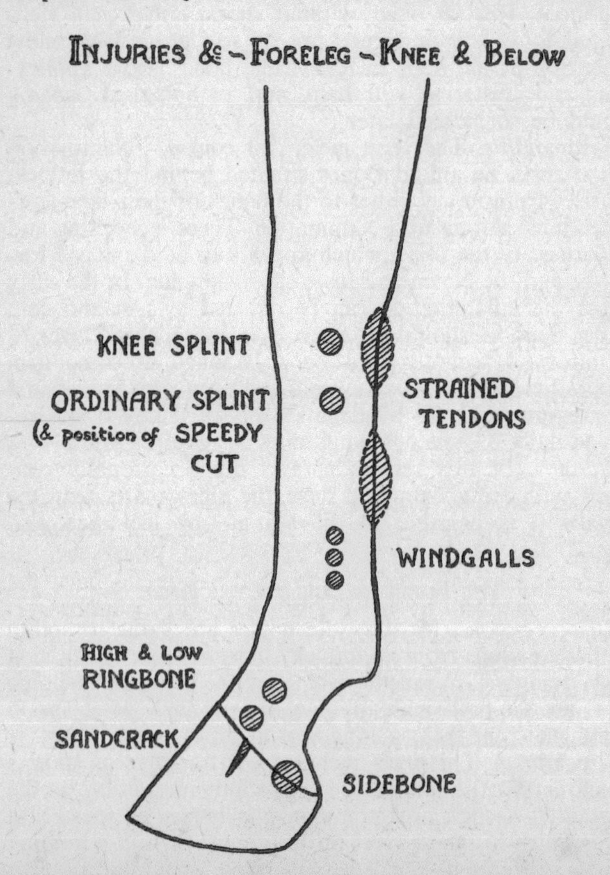

Splint Bone to the Cannon, is liable to follow inflammation to the covering membrane (Periosteum), caused by direct injury or concussion. Hereditary predisposition may be present. The enlargement is found usually on the inner side of the foreleg, either immediately under the knee—where it may "creep" and interfere with that joint—or anywhere between there and where the Splint Bone ends. It does occasionally form on the outside of the foreleg and even on the hind. Lameness is present in the early stages while the growth is developing but generally disappears when the two bones have finally joined. Many horses over five or six years old have splints which no longer cause trouble and are passed over as of no consequence. When the Splint cannot be seen or felt, it can be detected by the extreme tenderness of the part. Lameness shows best at the trot on hard ground. Treat as for sprains.

Windgalls. Small, soft swellings are common anywhere between the fetlock joints and the knees or hocks. They were given their name as, from their feel and appearance, they were at one time thought to contain air. These enlargements are fluid exuded from joint oil sacs, inflamed by concussion; many horses have them, particularly those working on hard ground, and lameness seldom accompanies them. A short rest, massage, and avoiding fast work on hard surfaces generally overcomes them or at least prevents their becoming hard and permanent.

THE FORELEG: THE KNEE AND ABOVE

Broken Knees. Broken knees are nearly always the result of a fall, and include, besides fractures of the bones, bruises and open wounds. It is possible there will be escape of joint oil, and it is well, therefore, to have the wound examined by an expert. Absolute cleanliness is essential, and to make removal of dirt easier the leg should be bent during cleansing. Antiseptic dressings should be used and inflammation reduced with cold water, which will also help in checking a flow of joint oil.

Knee Sprain. Knee Sprain also is generally the result of a fall. The part of the knee concerned can be determined by the degree of tenderness; there will probably also be stiffness, heat and swelling, and often the knee is broken. Treat as for sprains and broken knees.

Capped Elbow. The commonest cause of capped elbow, indicated by swelling, is long contact with hard surfaces—a bare patch of floor in the stable, or the shoe, when lying down. The swelling can be dispersed by hot or cold fomentations twice a day and precautions must be taken against recurrence. If insufficient bedding is not to blame, inspect the shoeing to see if the heels are too long. A method of prevention is an "elbow protector" or "preventer" also known as a "sausage boot"; this is a semicircular bolster-like pad easily made from materials at hand, or which can be bought from a saddler. It fits around the *pastern.*

Elbow Lameness. This may result from sprain, fracture or rheumatism and is shown by standing with the leg bent. Treatment must be directed to the particular cause.

Fractures. In the forearm there is the main bone, the Radius, with a smaller bone behind, the Ulna, which can be felt as a projection at the elbow. When one of these is fractured, the other may help as a natural splint, but the injury is serious. The usual signs of a break can be detected either at the front of the arm or at the back according to the bone affected. When applying splints, see that they are continued below the knee to prevent its movement.

Shoulder Lameness. Shoulder lameness may be brought on not only by injury, sprain, rheumatism, etc., but also by disorders of the stomach or liver. Symptoms are stiffness, dragging the toe, and an outward movement of the leg. They must be considered in conjunction with known facts and professional advice should always be sought. Injuries and sprains should have the usual cold water treatment, with a long rest. See also Rheumatism, page 143.

Fractures. (1) Humerus, or Arm Bone. This bone extends from the elbow to the Scapula, or Shoulder Blade, with which it forms the "Point of Shoulder". Fracture is exceptional and is usually set with a gutta percha splint kept in place by a wide bandage around the chest.

(2) Scapula (Shoulder Blade). This fracture can be detected by crepitation. The mass of muscle here is a protection, and keeps the broken parts in position when there is a fracture. A wide gutta percha splint should be bandaged over the Shoulder Blade, but slings may be required to take the weight.

The Hindleg

For trouble below the hock, see "The Foreleg: Below the Knee" and previous sections.

Monday Morning Leg. This term and "Big Leg" describe the condition more technically known as Lymphangitis (*not* epizootic). The names "Weed" and "A Shot of Grease" are also commonly used. The sufferers are usually hard-worked horses which have been idle for a day, and one or both hindlegs may be affected (or occasionally the forelegs). There is acute lameness, the limb is tender and painful and swells enormously in a short time. Other symptoms are fever and constipation. Improvement is noticed after two or three days' treatment, but the animal may continue lame for several more days. The pain can be relieved by hot water fomentations or hosing with cold water, and the constipation by ½ to 1 pint doses of Linseed Oil. Following the treatment, the legs benefit by the gentle application of embrocation. The diet should also be modified; bran mashes, green food, roots, etc., should be included and foods with a high protein content avoided. Short periods of walking exercise two or three times during the day, when the lameness has become less acute, complete the treatment. After recovery, ordinary feeding and work should be resumed gradually. Subsequently, prevention must be the aim. On non-working days feeding must be appropriate, the corn ration being reduced, and the animal should be given a little light exercise; it is always better, if conditions permit, to let a horse spend at least part of his off-duty day at grass rather than stand completely idle in the stable.

The Hock

Capped Hock. This is similar to Capped Elbow, with the same causes and prevention. Treatment is also similar, a "Hock Cap" being worn—a padded leather cover strapping around the *joint*—available from a saddler.

Curb. Curb is an enlargement at the back of the hock, due to sprain of tendons or ligaments from over-exertion, in jumping or galloping in deep, holding ground. It shows just below the point of the hock. Early treatment usually produces a cure with little difficulty, but neglect may lead to permanent enlargement and constant lameness. Rest,

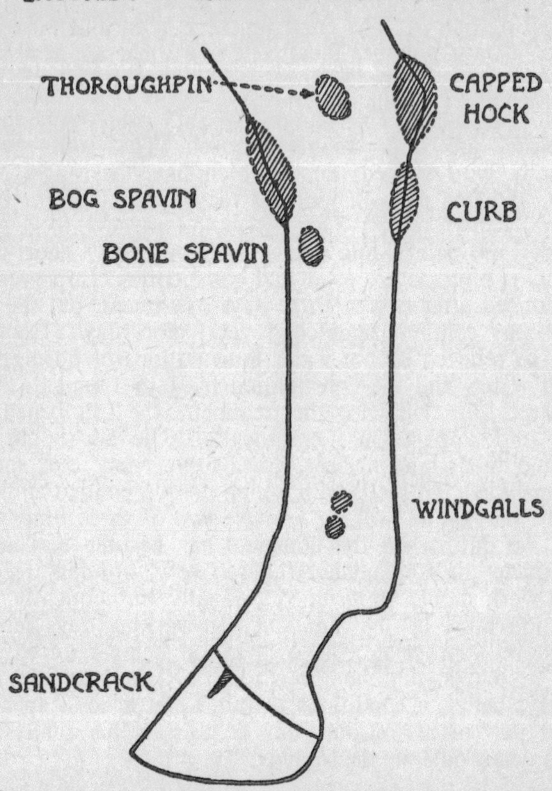

give laxative food, and cold applications to reduce inflammation. Blistering may be advised, and fitting shoes with calkins or high heels will relieve the leg of some strain.

Spavin. There are two kinds of Spavin. (1) "Bog" or "Blood". (2) "Bone". They occur as enlargements on the inside of the Hock Joint, usually from strain and probably hereditary tendency. Generally one hock only is affected, so the enlargement may be detected by comparison. The joint is stiff, and the toe of the shoe may be worn by dragging. A common method of testing is by well flexing the joints, bringing the foot up as close to the stifle as possible, then having the horse trotted away as soon as the foot is dropped, when lameness will be marked.

(1) Bog Spavin. The enlargement is soft, and lameness is not always present. Treatment is by massage, pressure and blistering; a special truss may be used for pressure, similar to a Thoroughpin Truss.

(2) Bone Spavin. The enlargement is hard and bony, and lameness results. Treatment is: rest and cold applications; massage with embrocation, or stronger blistering.

Sprained, or "Sprung" Hock. The Hock is often sprained in fast work, jumping or in heavy draught work. In minor cases only the ligaments are affected, but in others the bones and tendons may also be involved, and a sprung hock must always be regarded as requiring veterinary assistance. There is great pain, with tenderness and heat, and perhaps a high degree of fever. Prolonged, complete rest is necessary, with cold water treatment.

Thoroughpin. This is a fluid distension on either side of the hock, which can be pressed through to the other side by the finger—hence the old name, "Through-pin". Strain of some kind is the usual cause, but there is generally hereditary predisposition. Unless severe, the condition is not serious and there may be little or no lameness; it can be compared with Windgalls. With rest and massage the fluid will probably disperse, but sometimes it is drawn off surgically. High-heeled shoes give relief, or when standing in the stable the old method of pressure by a Thoroughpin Truss or a rubber bandage may be found effective.

Above the Hock

Stifle Lameness. Lameness in the stifle may be due to sprain, bruise of the joint, or, generally, dislocation of the patella, or knee-cap. The common causes are falling, twisting, strain when starting with a heavy load in draught, or stable accidents such as slipping, getting cast, turning in a narrow space and striking the joint against door jambs, etc. Young horses are often liable to slipped, or dislocated, stifle, but the patella is easily restored—usually by the natural action of the muscles. The lameness is shown by dragging the leg stiffly, with the toe scraping the ground, swelling and heat; the displaced bone can be seen as an enlargement on the outside of the stifle. Ordinary sprain should be treated in the usual way. Dislocation is corrected by passing a rope between the forelegs, around the pastern, and pulling forward until the foot is flat on the ground, while the horse is pushed back; the bone can then be pressed forward and downward and held in place while the horse is moved forward again, when it will "stay put". Skilled assistance should be obtained if possible.

Hip Joint. Sprain and injury cause lameness in this joint from similar causes as in Stifle Lameness. It may also be due to Rheumatism. There is difficulty in moving the leg, which appears shorter and is swung outwards with dragging of the toe; pain is severe and there is considerable heat and tenderness. If not from rheumatism, cold water brings relief, and a long rest should be given. High-heeled shoes are recommended. Very severe cases may have to be destroyed, if the muscles are badly torn.

22

Common ailments and injuries

Notifiable Diseases

There are certain "scheduled diseases" which the law requires to be notified to the police, the local authority or the Ministry of Agriculture's veterinary inspector. Although not common, they should be mentioned. These are: Anthrax, Parasitic Mange (see p. 161), Glanders or Farcy (see p. 163), Epizootic Lymphangitis and Rabies. The last three have been "controlled out of existence" in this country, and the first is rare, especially in horses.

Anthrax symptoms are seldom seen, the animal usually being found dead, often with bloody discharge from the natural openings of the body, although apparently healthy the previous day. In such circumstances the disease must be suspected and the case immediately reported; the carcase must not be touched.

Poisoning

Poisoning in horses is also rare, and when it does occur is usually from vegetable origin. Horses are less likely than other animals to eat poisonous plants, and whilst most cases can be traced to garden cuttings, nothing should be left to chance. Owners should thoroughly inspect new pasture, particularly hedges, as greediness for green food when first turned out, or during a dry summer, may lead to the animal exercising less than normal "choosiness" when grazing. At the risk of unpopularity, the attentions of passers-by should be firmly discouraged; more than one fatal case of poisoning has resulted from tit-bits accepted over the fence.

Dangerous Plants include: Yew, Laburnum, laurel, rhododendron, privet, boxwood, aconite (monkshood), foxglove, lupins, deadly nightshade, darnel (seeds), hellebore, hemlock, henbane and meadow saffron ("autumn crocus"). It is worth mentioning, however, that I have had horses which, although well-fed, showed great liking for privet and laurel, eating large quantities without ill-effects.

Symptoms. Except in the case of meadow saffron, the symptoms of poisoning show quickly, and according to whether the digestive or the nervous form is taken, the commonest are: Purging, excessive flow of saliva, dryness of the mouth, distension of the stomach, colic pains, feverish condition, giddiness, dilated pupils of the eyes, convulsions, stupor, paralysis, or loss of consciousness.

Treatment. Put the animal in a comfortable loose-box and send for professional assistance *immediately*, giving all relevant facts at the time, including, if possible, the nature of the poison. While waiting, the layman can take certain emergency measures. Any of the following will help:—

1. Frequent half-pint doses of strong black *boiled* coffee or tea.
2. Drenches of linseed tea, thin gruel, or barley water.
3. Encourage the horse to drink plenty of water; salt may be added to the food or water for this purpose.

Wounds and Injuries

Abscess. This is a swelling containing pus, caused by germs. For safety, the Veterinary Surgeon should be asked to give an anti-tetanus injection; he will probably also supply a tube of penicillin for daily injections into the wound. The abscess should be fomented continually to bring it to a pointed, soft "head", when it can be lanced, and subsequently dressed as a wound. (See also "Strangles".)

Galls. (1) Girth. Girth galls take the form of either swellings or soreness. The first is from tight girthing, the second from loose girthing, soft condition, or a hard girth. Swellings should be massaged, and rubs treated as ordinary wounds; in neither case should the horse be saddled again until the skin is normal. A useful dressing is a lotion made of Sugar of Lead and Sulphate of Zinc, 2 drs. of each mixed in 1½ pints of water. But prevention must be the aim. Some horses, owing to shape, gall easily; for these a safeguard is a wrapping of animal wool or a special sheepskin "sleeve" around the girth at the part rubbed. If the saddle continually slides forward, a crupper may help—that is, a strap buckled to the cantle and forming a loop for the tail. As most horses "blow themselves out" during girthing, note should be made of the advice on page 28.

(2) Saddle. Saddle galls also appear as either swellings or abrasions, from pressure or rubbing. Causes are badly-fitting saddles, slack girthing, and loose, unbalanced riding. The saddle must stay in the tack room until the back is cleared and then there must be no reason for recurrence. In the meantime, wound treatment can be given to abrasions (Gall Lotion), and swellings bathed with salt and water—one teaspoonful to a pint.

Mouth Injuries. These are usually found on the tongue, the corners of the lips, or the gums, and are caused by "ham-fisted" handling, badly-fitting bits, etc., and occasionally by sharp objects taken in with the food, a twig of hawthorn in the hay, for example. The essential part of the treatment is to hang up the bridle until the injury is *completely* healed—then be sure faults are corrected. When the tongue is cut, the mouth should be washed out after feeding, and boracic lotion will help. When eating is painful, soft food, such as bran, must be fed while the mouth is tender.

Wounds. For all wounds, however slight, it is wise to have a surgeon give an anti-tetanus injection as soon as possible.

In serious cases the first consideration is to stop bleeding, either by pressure bandaging above and below or directly over the wound. Then professional assistance must be obtained—stitching may be necessary.

In minor wounds, cleanliness is of greatest importance. There are many mild antiseptics suitable—solutions of any of the well-known brands are recommended (Jeyes Fluid, Lysol, etc.), in the proportions advised by the makers. Failing one of these, tincture of iodine, boracic powder, salt and water (one teaspoon to a pint of boiled water) or even plain, boiled water, can be used. Once the wound is clean, the aim is to dry it and therefore water should be used as little as possible. Bandages may have to be employed to keep out dirt, but it must be remembered that Nature alone heals wounds—sun and air are the finest agents. Sulphanilamide ointment is excellent, especially for deep wounds which can be plugged with it.

Note. In the following sections an unusual (and technically incorrect) system of listing complaints according to the most noticeable symptoms has been adopted with the object of assisting practical reference. For instance, a horse keeper may notice the signs of a cold and a thick discharge from one nostril, which to him do not, perhaps, indicate a "specific contagious disease", Glanders, but they do *appear to be respiratory symptoms; he is therefore able to turn to the appropriate section and trace the disease far more quickly than if he had to wade through the complete chapter, comparing the symptoms of all complaints.*

Ailments with Skin and Coat Symptoms

Eczema. There are two forms of this skin disease, moist and dry. The former is more common in the horse and is shown by itchiness and discharge which causes matting of the hair. In the dry form the hair falls out, leaving grey scales and thickening and wrinkling of the skin. These symptoms may lead to confusion with mange, and microscopic examination is necessary to differentiate, therefore the Veterinary Surgeon should be called in. Digestive disorders are usually concerned, aided by dirty conditions, and treatment must be directed towards these causes. The corn ration should be reduced, and green food, bran mashes, etc., included in the diet. Clip the hair from the affected parts and wash these with a safe disinfectant. (See also "Mallenders".)

Farcy. A skin form of Glanders. See pages 157 and 163.

Lice. Two types are found on horses—biting and sucking lice, the latter usually infesting the roots of long hair, such as the mane and tail. Both thrive in dirty conditions but may be transferred to clean animals via buildings, trees, etc. The horse becomes poor and suffers from itchiness and loss of coat, and the insects can be detected when the coat is parted. Cleanliness of the animal and his surroundings is the best preventive, and the parasites can quickly be cleared by "Gammexane" dusted thoroughly into the coat and worked down into the roots with the fingers. Two applications at intervals of seven days should be sufficient to kill the insects and later-hatching eggs. Everything that has had contact with the horse, from buildings (particularly woodwork) to grooming kit, should be disinfected. Horse lice cannot live on man; the fleas of other domestic animals and the lice of humans are not found on the horse.

Mallenders and Sallenders. These are eczematious affections of the back of the knee and the front of the hock respectively, and are frequently hereditary. The skin becomes inflamed and cracked or raw, the bending of the joints tending to keep it open. There may be some temporary lameness for this reason. Dissolve a little washing soda in warm water and wash the parts with this and hard soap; dry thoroughly and rub in zinc or iodine ointment. Continue this treatment for some days after apparent healing.

Mange. (See also page 157.) For practical purposes this parasitic skin disease may be divided into two forms—dry and moist. Although there are exceptions, all cases should be regarded as highly contagious to other animals, *including man,* and skilled attention must be obtained. Under the Parasitic Mange Order the disease must be notified to the police. Almost any part of the horse may be affected, including the inside of the ears.

In the dry form the parasites burrow beneath the skin, but affect only the surface in the moist.

The symptoms are severe irritation, shedding of the hair in patches, the formation of small pimples, scabs or ulcers, or hardening and furrowing of the skin. In serious cases there is rapid falling away in condition, followed by death.

The owner's part in treatment must be to prevent the disease spreading—by strict isolation and thorough disinfection.

Nettlerash. In this minor complaint the only symptoms are flat swellings of varying sizes which suddenly appear, irregularly scattered over the body, and disappear in a matter of hours. These swellings are similar to those we get from contact with stinging nettles.

It may be due to bad management, such as errors in feeding, lack of exercise, or chills on returning hot from work. Bites and stings are also causes.

Little treatment is necessary; prevention is the answer. A bran mash is helpful, but general management should be overhauled and the diet may need changing—check up on the protein content, it may be excessive for the work. If the trouble can be pinned to chilling, allow the horse to cool after work before watering, or avoid very cold water.

Ringworm. This is a parasitic skin disease in which a fungus grows at the roots of the hair, which becomes matted and falls out to disclose scurfy patches of skin covered with grey scales. These areas gradually increase in size and merge into other patches. Bad management, dirty conditions, etc., are the usual causes.

In treatment, remember the disease is contagious to humans as well as other animals, therefore isolation and disinfection are necessary. The hair surrounding the patches must be clipped off to check spreading, scabs removed with soap and water, then tincture of iodine or iodine ointment applied twice a week to the exposed skin and its edges is sufficient. If the patches are large it is advisable to deal with small portions each day.

Ailments with respiratory Symptoms

In infectious respiratory conditions, nursing, strict isolation and disinfection are important. As a further precaution against the spread of germs, frequent spraying of the stables with a recognised antiseptic is recommended.

Coughs and Colds. These and sore throat are often found together. In colds, or catarrh, there is a watery discharge from the nose, and perhaps some fever; when accompanied by cough there is usually soreness of the throat and difficulty in swallowing. The most common causes are similar to the human ones—sudden chilling, draughts, etc. Coughs may also be due to dusty forage, or, when chronic, to worms.

The particular causes should have attention. Rubbing the throat with embrocation and steaming the head with medicated vapour afford relief (see end of chapter). Chlorodyne and glycerine, at the rate of ½ oz. of each, may be given in the food twice daily for a week. For a bad cough it is advisable to give easily swallowed food, and linseed tea is useful.

Broken Wind. This is the term given to a chronic respiratory condition (pulmonary emphysema), characterised by a deep, persistent cough which is present even at rest and is often most marked when the horse is feeding. The reduced efficiency of the lungs results in an exaggerated expiratory movement of the chest and a characteristic "catching up" of the belly muscles, producing a pronounced furrow or groove —the so-called "broken winded furrow". The condition can be alleviated by decreasing bulk, increasing concentrates and adopting a clean air policy in the stable of reducing dust by dampening hay and feeds.

Bronchitis. This is a chest infection with inflammation of the bronchial tubes, and can be diagnosed from the noise made in breathing, and the painful cough. The causes are similar to those of colds, pneumonia, etc.

The horse should be put into a comfortable, well-ventilated loose-box, and professional aid obtained. The nostrils may be steamed with medicated vapour.

Glanders. (See page 157.) This dangerous, contagious disease, which may be passed on to humans, must be reported to the police. It is due to a bacterial organism which enters the body via contaminated food, through the skin by cuts, grazes, etc., or, less often, by inhalation. The usual symptoms of a chill are present, and small nodules form in the nose (which may be swollen), later breaking into ulcers. There is often a sticky discharge, generally from one nostril, and a hard "fixed" lump appears under the jaw on this side. Condition deteriorates rapidly and death usually follows in a week or two. In the chronic form, most common in the horse, the only early stages may be slight fever. In the skin form, "Farcy", similar ulcers ("Farcy Buds") form in a row on the inside of the legs and sometimes on the head and neck.

Isolation and disinfection are essential. The presence of the disease can be detected in possible contacts by the "Mallein" test; reactors are slaughtered.

Bovine Farcy has no connection with Glanders.

Influenza. ("Pink Eye".) This is an epizootic (animal epidemic) infectious fever. The animal generally "goes off his feed", loses flesh rapidly and becomes very weak. There is often catarrhal discharge from the nose and eyes and the latter may become swollen and inflamed.

Good nursing is the best treatment; the patient must be isolated in a comfortable draught-free loose-box and kept warm with rugs and leg bandages. Every effort must be made to tempt his appetite and keep up his strength. Steaming the nostrils is of benefit. After recovery, a long rest will be required.

Equine influenza is *not* communicable to man.

Pleurisy. Inflammation of the lining of the chest. See "Pneumonia".

Pneumonia. Inflammation of the lungs may follow a cold, and should be treated as contagious to other horses. There is loss of appetite and rapid loss of flesh; fever, with inflammation of the lining of the eyes, a fast pulse and quickened breathing; constipation, and often a reddish discharge from the nose, and a cough. Usually the animal stands with his forelegs apart, and if the ribs are tapped over the lungs a dull sound is heard.

The essential treatment is good nursing with attention to general comfort and efforts to tempt the appetite (green food is valuable). Relief will be obtained from hot blankets to the chest, and small doses of linseed oil (½ pint). A long rest should follow recovery.

Roaring. When the larynx muscles are affected, following chest complaints, often from hereditary predisposition, a characteristic whistling or roaring noise is made in deep breathing—as during or following hard exercise. Little can be done; treatment for sore throat may be tried, but in bad cases an operation is necessary. "Hobdaying" or "Tubing" is generally resorted to; this is the insertion of a tube into the windpipe to facilitate breathing.

Strangles. This serious and contagious fever, which more commonly affects youngsters, involving the glands of the neck, is typified by abscesses at the throat, between the branches of the jaw. There is lack of appetite, loss of flesh, and catarrhal symptoms with cough and difficulty in swallowing.

Isolation and disinfection are necessary. The patient should be encouraged to eat well, and constipation must be avoided; the diet should include green food, roots, bran mashes and a generous supply of linseed gruel. Steaming the nostrils with medicated vapour is beneficial. When the abscesses burst or are opened, the discharge must be destroyed.

The disease is *not* communicable to man.

Whistling. A form of Roaring.

NOTE

Inhalations

In many of the foregoing complaints steaming the nostrils is recommended. These inhalations are prepared by pouring boiling water over a handful of chaff, bran or hay in a nosebag; the vapour can be medicated by adding a teaspoonful of Friar's Balsam, spirits of camphor, terebene, etc. The nosebag should be worn for 10 to 15 minutes three times daily. A bucket may be used, with a blanket or sack loosely surrounding the nose to gain full benefit from the vapour but to admit some air as well.

AILMENTS WITH DIGESTIVE SYMPTOMS

Colic. Colic, or Gripes, might be likened to severe indigestion or "tummy-ache". Pain is obviously intense, shown by sweating, constant pawing, turning the head towards the belly or striking at it with a hindfoot. There may be drum-like distension (flatulent colic), and the animal shows signs of distress and uneasiness. In severe cases he often lies down and rises repeatedly, and may roll continually—when there is danger of twisting or knotting of the intestines. Bad management, especially in feeding, is the common cause, working when exhausted, drinking after a full feed, etc. Worms are sometimes the trouble.

In view of the possible seriousness of colic, and its resemblance to Inflammation of the Bowels in cause and symptoms, it is always safer to call the Veterinary Surgeon. It is often recommended that, in the meantime, the horse should be walked about to avoid rolling, but this must depend upon the severity of the case. If an animal is exhausted it is obviously foolish to keep him on the move; a rest often eases him, but he should be kept under observation to prevent complications. Severe cases obtain relief from hot blankets to the belly. When available, two wine-glassfuls of brandy, gin or whisky (with three parts water) allay pain in the spasmodic type. Minor cases of the flatulent forms are best treated with a mild laxative, such as ½ to 1 pint of Linseed Oil. Bran mashes are advisable for a time.

Constipation. The usual causes of this are unsuitable food, sudden changes in diet—as when first brought in from grass, etc. The condition can be corrected by the diet, by including bran mashes and green food. ½ to 1 pint doses of Linseed Oil should be given as a laxative.

Diarrhœa. Frequent causes are bad management and feeding, overwork, sudden changes in diet, etc. Find the cause and correct it; include dry bran in the food, and give gruel or linseed jelly. A ½ to 1 pint dose of Castor Oil helps by clearing irritation from this part of the system.

Stomach and Bowel Inflammations. Under this heading

are included Enteritis (inflammation of the bowels), Peritonitis (inflammation of the lining of the belly) and Gastritis (inflammation of the stomach), as it is difficult for the layman to distinguish between them. Symptoms, causes and treatment are generally similar to those for Colic. While waiting for the Veterinary Surgeon, woollen blankets should be wrung out in hot water and applied to the belly, being renewed frequently to retain warmth. Linseed Oil and Laudanum are usually given internally in small doses, and by injecting morphine derivatives.

Worms. Many types of worms are found in the horse, the most common being the long white and the needle worms. When they exist in any number the animal loses condition badly and cannot improve until the parasites are cleared. A harsh, staring coat is frequently the sign of internal parasites, which may or may not be noticed in the droppings.

Feed bran mashes for a day or two, then, after a night's fast, give a draught of from ½ to 1 pint of Linseed Oil with ½ to 1 oz. of Turpentine, according to size. This drench may have to be given once a week for three or four weeks; a day's rest should follow each draught. In cases of doubt or difficulty, obtain a veterinary prescription.

Liver Disorders

The general symptoms of liver disorders are: a yellowish tinge in the membranes, loss of appetite, constipation, sour breath, raised temperature, and sometimes tenderness of the right side and lameness of that foreleg. Causes are various—parasites, mismanagement (bad feeding, and unventilated stables), want of green food, influenza, glanders, etc. Treatment must be according to the cause, but a dose of 3 ozs. of Epsom Salts in a mash or the drinking water for three or four days helps.

Simple Weights and Measures

1 Teaspoon	⅛ oz. or 1 drachm.
2 Teaspoons... ...	1 dessertspoon.
2 Dessertspoons ...	1 tablespoon (½ oz. or 4 drachms).
4 Tablespoons ...	1 wineglass (2 ozs.).
3 Wineglasses ...	1 teacup (6 ozs.).
1 Breakfast Cup or Tumbler ...	10 ozs. or ½ pint.

APPENDIX 1

COLOURS AND MARKINGS OF HORSES

Reproduced by permission of the Royal College of Veterinary Surgeons, and the National Veterinary Medical Association of Great Britain and Ireland.

Owing to variations in nomenclature of colours and markings in different parts of the country, and in different breeds of horses, descriptions by different persons of the same horse have been found to vary very considerably.

The following list of names of colours and marking is recommended as sufficient. Popular names not included below are recommended to be discontinued:—

COLOURS

Black.

Melanistic pigment general throughout body coat, limbs, mane and tail, with no pattern factor present other than white markings.

Black-Brown.

Predominating colour black, with muzzle, and sometimes flanks, brown or tan.

Brown.

Mixture of melanistic and chocolate pigment, without yellow, in the body coat.

Bay-Brown.

Predominating colour brown, muzzle bay.

Bay.

Bay varies considerably in shade, from a dull red approaching brown, to a yellowish colour approaching chestnut. Almost invariably black on the limbs. The following three shades will suffice:—*Bay* (includes bright bay); *Dark Bay, Light Bay* (includes mealy bay).

Chestnut.

Whole colour, of which three shades may be named:—

Chestnut:—Includes bright chestnut, golden chestnut, and red chestnut.

Dark Chestnut:—Includes liver chestnut and mahogany chestnut.

Light Chestnut:—Includes sorrel.

Blue Dun.

Colour of body coat a dilute black evenly distributed (giving a blue colour) with or without dorsal band (list) or withers stripe. Always a black mane and tail. Skin black.

Yellow Dun.

A diffuse yellow pigment in hair, with or without dorsal band (list), withers stripes, or bars on legs. Striping is correlated with dark pigment on head and limbs. When striping absent the limbs will approximate to the colour of the body coat. Skin black.

Cream.

Body coat of a cream colour, with unpigmented skin. Iris deficient in pigment, it may be devoid of it, giving the eye a pinkish appearance.

Grey.

Body coat a varying mosaic of black and white hair, with skin black. With increasing age the coat grows lighter in colour. There are many variations of grey, according to age and season. In horses of this colour any distinctive hoof markings may be useful for purposes of identification.

Roans.

Roans are distinguished by ground or body colours all of which are permanent:—

Blue Roan:—Body colour black or black brown, with an admixture of white hair, giving a blue tinge to the coat.

Bay or Red Roan:—Body colour bay or bay brown with admixture of white hairs, giving a reddish tinge to coat.

Strawberry or Chestnut Roan:—Body colour chestnut with an admixture of white hairs.

Piebald.

Body coat consists of large irregular patches of black and white. Line of demarcation between the two colours generally well defined.

Skewbald.

Body coat consists of large irregular patches of white

and of any definite colour, except black. Line of demarcation between colours generally well defined.

Odd Coloured.

Coat consists of mixture of more than two colours tending to merge into each other at the edges of the patches, with irregular body markings not classifiable under head of Piebald or Skewbald.

NOTE. (1) Where there is any doubt as to the colour, the muzzle and eyes should be carefully examined.

(2) The term "whole coloured" is used where there are no hairs of any other colour on the body, head or limbs.

MARKINGS

Variation in markings of horses are infinite, and cannot therefore be comprehended by a limited number of terms without certain arbitrary groupings. In some cases, a combination of terms given below must be resorted to:—

LIMBS

White Coronet.

Hair immediately above the hoof, white.

White Heel.

Heel to be taken as the back of the pastern extending to the ergot. Where white is confined to one or both the bulbs of the heel, it must be so specified.

White Pastern.

Term "Pastern" to be taken as extending from immediately below the fetlock joint downwards. Any variation of the extent of the white should be specified, *viz.*, half pastern, three-quarter pastern.

White Fetlock.

Term "Fetlock" comprising the region of the fetlock joint and downwards. Any variation of the white should be specified.

Higher White Markings.

The term "sock" has been in common use for a marking extending to about halfway up the cannon, and the term "stocking" for a marking up to the region of the knee or hock, but these terms have been so loosely used that for the sake of greater uniformity and certainty, it is recommended that for white markings extending higher than those already defined, the particular height to which the white extends should be precisely stated, and any variation in the upper margin noted, *viz.*, "White to middle of cannon or shank," "White to knee or hock".

Head

Star.

Any white mark on forehead. Size, shape, intensity, position and coloured markings on white to be specified.

Stripe.

Many terms have been used to describe the narrow white marking down the face, not wider than the flat anterior surface of the nasal bones, *viz.*, rase, race, rache, reach, streak, stripe, strip, etc. One term only should be used, and, as being most useful for the purpose, the term "stripe" should be used. The stripe may be a continuation of the star, or it may be separate and distinct from it. Where there is a star and the stripe is not continuous with it, the stripe should be described as "interrupted stripe", and where star and stripe are continuous, as "a star and stripe conjoined"; where no star, the origin of the stripe should be defined. The termination of the stripe and any variation in breadth, length, direction and coloured markings on the white should be described, *viz.*, "broad stripe", "narrow stripe".

Blaze.

White marking covering almost the whole of the forehead between the eyes, and extending down the front of the face, involving the whole width of the nasal bones. Any variation in direction, termination and coloured markings on the white should be described.

White Face.

Where white covers the forehead and front of face, extending laterally towards the mouth. The extension may be unilateral or bilateral, in which case it should be described accordingly.

Snip.

Isolated white marking, situated between, or in the region of the nostrils. Its position should be specified.

Lip Markings.

Should be accurately described, whether embracing the whole or a portion of either lip.

White Muzzle.
Where the white embraces both lips and nostrils to the region of the nostrils.

EYES

Wall-Eye.
Used exclusively where there is a lack of pigment in the iris as usually to give a greyish-white or bluish-white appearance to the eye. Any important variations from the normal colour of the iris should be noted.

Showing the White of the Eye.
Horses which "show the white of the eye" should be so described.

BODY

Grey-Ticked.
Isolated white hairs sparsely distributed through the coat in any part of the body.

Flecked.
Small collections of white hairs distributed irregularly in any part of the body. The degree of flecking may be described by the terms "heavily flecked", "lightly flecked".

Black Marks.
Used to describe small areas of black hairs on white or any other colour (see "Ermine marks").

Spots.
Small, more or less circular, collection of hairs differing from the general body colour, distributed in various parts of the body. The colour of the spots must be stated.

Patch.
Used to describe any larger well defined irregular area (not covered by previous definitions) of hairs differing from the general body colour. The colour, shape, position and extent should be described.

Zebra Marks.
Striping on the limbs, neck, withers or quarters.

Mane and Tail.
The presence of odd-coloured hairs in mane and tail should be specified.

Ermine Marks.

Used to describe black points on white, usually occurring on the coronet, but as this marking can easily be described as "Black Marks", it is recommended that the use of the word "Ermine" is discontinued.

Dappled.

It is recommended that this term be discontinued, as it is a seasonal and not a permanent marking.

General

Mixed.

Used to describe a marking consisting of the general colour mixed with many white or lighter coloured hairs.

Bordered.

Used where any marking is circumscribed by a mixed border, *viz.*, bordered star, bordered stripe.

Flesh Marks.

Patches where the Pigment of the skin is absent should be described as "Flesh Marks".

Notes

Adventitious Marks.

There are many adventitious marks (*viz.*, *not* congenital marks), which are permanent, *viz.*, saddle marks, bridle marks, girth marks and other harness marks, permanent bandage marks, firing and branding marks, scars, tattoo marks. Wherever these occur they should be described. Horses that have been docked should be so described.

Near and Off.

As the terms "Near" and "Off" are not recognised abroad, it is recommended that in certificates referring to horses for export, an explanatory note telling "near" as left, and "off" as right, should be inserted at the foot of the certificate.

APPENDIX 2

PERIODICALS OF INTEREST

"*Horse and Hound*", 189 High Holborn, London, WC1V 7BA. Mainly for hunting and racing folk, but invaluable to every horseman who wishes to keep up to date.

"*Light Horse*"; "*Pony*". The Publishers of these excellent magazines, D. J. Murphy (Publishers) Ltd., 19 Charing Cross Road, London, W.C.2, have kindly provided many of the delightful photographs in this book.

"*Riding*", 189 High Holborn, London, WC1V 7BA. Monthly. An interesting and instructive magazine for horse-lovers of all ages.

In addition, of course, the many sporting, agricultural country and animal protection societies' journals are of interest to the horse-owner.

HORSE AND PONY ASSOCIATIONS, SOCIETIES, ETC.

Ada Cole Memorial Stables, Broadlands, Broadley Common, Nr. Nazeing, Essex, also Secretary (Mrs. D. Hedges), 2 Gleneagle Road (off Streatham High Road), London, S.W.16.
Ancient Order of Pack Riders (Mrs. J. M. Williams), Brookfield Cottage, Venlake Cross, Uplyme, Lyme Regis, Dorset.
Animal Health Trust (Leslie T. Neck, M.C., T.D.), 232-235 Abbey House, Victoria Street, London, S.W.1.
Arab Horse Society (Brig. F. H. V. Purcell, M.B.E.), Loughmoe, Shelley Close, Itchen Abbas, Hants.
Association of British Riding Schools, The Moat House, Alconbury Hill, Hunts.
Association of Masters of Harriers and Beagles (J. J. Kirkpatrick), Little Rissington Manor, Glos.
British Bloodstock Agency, 26 Charing Cross Road, London, W.C.1.
British Driving Society (L. H. Candler), Little Phaeton, The Pentagon, Fawley, Hants.
British Field Sports Society, 137 Victoria Street, London, S.W.1.
British Horse Society, National Equestrian Centre, Stoneleigh, Kenilworth, Warwicks.
British Palomino Society (Mrs. Peter Howell), Cholderton, Salisbury, Wilts.
British Percheron Horse Society (A. E. Vyse), Owen Webb House, Gresham Road, Cambridge.
British Show Hack and Cob Association (John E. Blackmore), National Equestrian Centre, Stoneleigh, Kenilworth, Warwicks.
British Show Jumping Association (Capt. G. H. S. Webber), National Equestrian Centre, Stoneleigh, Kenilworth, Warwicks.
British Show Pony Society (Capt. R. P. Grellis), Smale Farm, Wisborough Green, Billingshurst, Sussex.
British Spotted Horse Society (Miss Joan Eddie), Nashend, Bisley, Stroud, Glos.
British Veterinary Association, 7 Mansfield Street, London, W.1.
Cherry Tree Farm Home of Rest, Newchapel, Nr. Lingfield, Surrey.
Cleveland Bay Horse Society (J. F. Stephenson), York Livestock Centre, Murton, York.
Clydesdale Horse Society (Stewart Gilmore, C.A.), 24 Beresford Terrace, Ayr.
Coaching Club (R. A. Brown), 65 Medfield Street, Roehampton, S.W.15.
Commons, Open Spaces and Footpath Preservation Society, 166 Shaftesbury Avenue, London, W.C.2.

Connemara Pony Breeders' Society (John Killeen), 4 Nun's Island, Galway, Eire.
Dales Pony Society (P. A. Lawson), Cleveland House, Hutton Gate, Guisborough, Yorks.
Dartmoor Pony Society (Dr. Roberts), Lower Hisley, Lustleigh, Nr. Newton Abbot, Devon.
English Connemara Pony Society (Mrs. Barthorp), The Quinta, Bentley, Farnham, Surrey.
Exmoor Pony Society (Miss J. Head), Styles Cottages, Rodhuish, Minehead.
F.E.I. (Fédèration Equestre Internationale) (Chevalier H. de Menten de Horne), Avenue Hamoir, 38 Bruxelles 18, Belgium.
Fell Pony Society (Miss Crossland), Packway, Windermere, Westmorland.
"The Field", 8 Stratton Street, London, W.1.
General Stud Book (Weatherby & Sons), Sanders Road, Wellingborough, Northants, NN8 4BX.
Hackney Horse Society (Major G. A. Worboys), 35 Belgrave Square, London, S.W.1.
The Highland Pony Society (James R. McIldowie), 51/53 High Street, Dunblane, Perths.
Home of Rest for Horses, Westcroft Stables, Speen, Nr. Aylesbury, Bucks.
Horse and Hound, 189 High Holborn, London, WC1V 7BA.
Horse and Pony Benefit Fund (Miss J. Firmin), 3 Caenwood, Ashstead Wood Road, Ashstead, Surrey.
Horse and Ponies Protection Association, 1 Station Parade, Balham, London, S.W.12.
Hunters' Improvement and National Light Horse Breeding Society (G. Evans), 17 Devonshire Street, London, W.1.
Hunt Secretaries' Association (Major G. Dobson), Babcary Old Rectory, Somerton, Somerset.
Hunt Servants' Benefit Society (D. A. Wright), The Council Offices Annexe, Storrington, Pulborough, Sussex.
Hurlingham Polo Association (Brig. J. R. C. Gannon, C.B.E., M.V.O.), 2/4 Idol Lane, London, E.C.3.
International League for the Protection of Horses (Mrs. M. F. Colvin, M.B.E.), 4 Bloomsbury Square, London, W.C.1.
Jockey Club, 42 Portman Square, London, W.1.
Joint Measurement Scheme (J. E. Blackmore), National Equestrian Centre, Stoneleigh, Kenilworth, Warwicks.
London Harness Horse Parade Society (R. A. Brown), 65 Medfield St., Roehampton, S.W.15.
Master Saddlers Ltd., The Society of, 9 St. Thomas Street, London, S.E.1.
National Farmers' Union, Agriculture House, 25/31 Knightsbridge, London, S.W.1.
National Farmers' Union of Scotland (H. G. Munroe, M.A., LL.B., W.S.), 17 Grosvenor Crescent, Edinburgh, EH12 5EN.
National Master Farriers and Blacksmiths and Agricultural Engineers Association, 48 Spencer Place, Leeds, 7.
National Master Farriers and Blacksmiths Association, 48 Spencer Place, Leeds, 7.

National Pony Society (Cmdr. B. H. Brown), Stoke Lodge, 85 Cliddesden Road, Basingstoke, Hants.
National Veterinary Medical Association of Great Britain and Ireland, 36 Gordon Square, London, W.C.1.
New Forest Pony Breeding and Cattle Society (Miss D. Macnair), Beacon Corner, Burley, Ringwood, Hants.
Our Dumb Friends League (inc.) The Blue Cross Animal Hospital, Hugh Street, London, S.W.1.
People's Dispensary for Sick Animals of the Poor, P.D.S.A. Sanatorium, Woodford Bridge, Redbridge, Ilford, Essex.
Ponies of Britain Club (Mrs. Glenda Spooner), Brookside Farm, Ascot, Berks.
Royal Veterinary College, Royal College Street, Camden Town, London, N.W.1.
Shetland Pony Breeders Club (Miss N. du Port), Tanglewood, Liss, Hants.
Shetland Pony Stud Book Society (Duncan M. Patterson), 8 Whinfield Road, Montrose, Angus.
Shire Horse Society (R. W. Bird), The Showground, Alwalton, Peterborough, PE2 OXE, Northants.
Show and Breed Secretaries' Association (E. Dillamore), 35 Belgrave Square, London, S.W.1.
South Wales and Monmouthshire Horse Show Association, 131-141 Crwys Road, Cardiff.
Sport and General Press Agency, 2 Gough Square, London, E.C.4.
Suffolk Horse Society (W. J. Woods), 6 Church Street, Woodbridge, Suffolk.
Thoroughbred Breeders Assoc., F. E. Birch, Esq., 26 Bloomsbury Way, London, W.C.1.
Welsh Pony & Cob Society, T. E. Roberts, Esq., 32 North Parade, Aberystwyth, Cards.

INDEX

S.

T.

U.

V.

W.

Z

LEARNING TO DRIVE IN PICTURES

by A. Tom Topper

The *first* book to really *attack* the difficulties simply and logically. The first quarter of this 208-page book—teaches absolute mastery of car control *to be* practised on open spaces or quiet, safe back streets. Step-by-step methods for achieving perfect three point turns, reverses into openings and hill starts (the three major bugbears) are all taught BEFORE throwing you in the deep end of thick traffic.

Many have been frightened off learning to drive by appalling instruction and trying to learn things far out of their depth to begin with. A few awful frights and the whole project seems to become a hysterical nightmare. All this can be avoided with Tom Topper, the master teacher.

THE AUTHOR DIAGNOSES DANGER MET IN DRIVING

THE ESSENTIAL MASTER-DRIVING LIFE-SAVING POINTS are not glossed over and ignored—each is emphasized and explained, so that a child of 12 could understand.

Wonderful reviews appeared on publication and here are some extracts:

The Times: 'Down-to-earth . . . practical . . . basic'

Daily Telegraph: 'For those who are still struggling . . . good value'

Daily Mirror: 'Clearer than many more expensive manuals'

The Sun: 'Admirable . . . amazingly cheap . . . invaluable'

Daily Sketch: 'Easiest to understand . . . excellent'

Woman's Own: 'Very helpful . . . gives all the theory'

More publicity was accorded when the 2nd edition appeared by the *Daily Mail*, *Woman's Own* again and London *Evening News*, etc.

The enormous 1st edition of six figures was sold within months under our famous 'Test pass or money back guarantee'. We had none returned.

Uniform with this volume